Stop Selling and Start Caring

Stop Selling
and
Start Caring

By
Michael S. Miller

E-BookTime, LLC
Montgomery, Alabama

Stop Selling and Start Caring

ISBN: 978-1-60862-293-1

First Edition
Published June 2011
E-BookTime, LLC
6598 Pumpkin Road
Montgomery, AL 36108
www.e-booktime.com

Contents

Preface

What Does it Mean to Sell at Combat Speed?

The word *combat* in any context sounds harsh, right? When I speak at conferences, I am frequently asked to change the title of my presentation, *Selling at Combat Speed*, because *combat* seems too harsh. But allow me to explain.

I have never known an organization that trains and prepares individuals the way the U.S. military does. A soldier is trained to act without thinking. Wow, did I really just say that? You see, in a life or death situation, if a soldier has to stop and think about the training he received, he may lose his life or cause the loss of other lives. But we are talking about salespeople in Corporate America, not soldiers . . . right? Correct! But whether you are in combat, Corporate America, or professional sports, the same methodology applies. If a wide receiver has to stop and think about all the tasks involved in making a catch, he will more than likely miss the ball. He may not even see the ball coming at him. If a golfer has to think about the mechanics that go into a perfect swing, his golf shot will be as inconsistent as mine is. If a salesperson has to stop and think about the steps of the sales process or the questions he needs to ask, he will not be focused on the prospect, but on what he is going to say next. In any profession, to perform effectively, we have to commit these processes to muscle memory. They must become habits. We should not have to think about them. They should just happen. That's what it means to sell at combat speed.

As salespeople, we need to take ownership of our sales process. We will follow the guidelines of the P-Effect, the system being taught in this book, but each of us will make it unique, to suit his or her personal style. How does this happen? First, trainers need to lose the scripts. Salespeople need to be taught a process, and coaching should be implemented to assist each salesperson to develop a unique sales process based on that person's style. The questions that I feel comfortable asking could make you very uncomfortable. But we can change the *way* we ask the question to gather the same information. Ninety-nine percent of the time, a salesperson will not ask a question that makes him or her uncomfortable. Asking the right question at the right time requires skill, even more so if the question that needs to be asked takes the salesperson out of the comfort zone.

So, what does it mean to be a sales warrior and to sell at combat speed? It starts with a major shift in mentality. If we take the same approach to our sales process as a soldier does to his rifle, what will the impact be? First of all, we have to understand what that rifle means to the soldier. Here is *The Rifleman's Creed:*

> *This is my rifle. There are many like it, but this one is mine. My rifle is my best friend. It is my life. I must master it as I must master my life. My rifle, without me, is useless. Without my rifle, I am useless. I must fire my rifle true. I must shoot straighter than my enemy who is trying to kill me. I must shoot him before he shoots me. I will . . .*

My rifle and myself know that what counts in this war is not the rounds we fire, the noise of our burst, nor the smoke we make. We know that it is the hits that count. We will hit...

My rifle is human, even as I, because it is my life. Thus, I will learn it as a brother. I will learn its weaknesses, its strength, its parts, its accessories, its sights and its barrel. I will ever guard it against the ravages of weather and damage as I will ever guard my legs, my arms, my eyes and my heart against damage. I will keep my rifle clean and ready. We will become part of each other. We will . . .

Before God, I swear this creed. My rifle and myself are the defenders of my country. We are the masters of our enemy. We are the saviors of my life. So be it, until victory is America's, and there is no enemy, but peace!

If you are thinking that I have seen too much combat and have completely lost my mind, I ask for just a few more minutes of your time before you close this book. Imagine for a minute if you developed a creed for your sales process. Maybe it would look very similar to mine, where I have changed a few words of *The Rifleman's Creed* to make it my own.

This is my sales process. There are many like it, but this one is mine. My sales process is my best friend. It is my life. I must master it as I must master my life. My sales process, without me, is useless. Without my sales process, I am useless. I must show

I care for my prospect more than my competitor who does not care at all. I must and I will care.

I know that what counts the most is not the number of deals I close, the amount of money I make, nor the competitions I win. I know that it is my integrity and the number of people I help. I must and I will help.

My sales process is alive, even as I, because it is my life. Thus, I will learn it as a brother. I will learn its weaknesses, its strength, its capabilities, and its failures. I will ever guard it against the ravages of those who have no integrity, as I will ever guard my legs, my arms, my eyes, and my heart against damage. I will refine, maintain, and continue to master my sales process. We will become part of each other. We will become one.

If you truly believe and live by this creed, how will it change your life? I know it will impact the way you sell and the activities you perform every day. I know you will move toward a more customer-focused selling process. I know that you will increase your closing ratio immensely. However, most will not even attempt to make this commitment. Most will remain content to be average salespeople; after all, average means being among the majority. The minority will step up to the plate and commit to a new and more dynamic way to do the job. They will do what others will not, and that is why they will succeed. These few will learn to sell at combat speed and become sales warriors.

So, I ask you right now, are you ready to make a commitment? Are you ready to be the change that needs to happen? Are you ready to do the things that others will not do?

STOP RIGHT NOW! Make your choice.

Whether you choose to make the commitment or not, you are going to benefit from this book. Some of you will learn enough to make minor changes. A small handful of you will make the full commitment. Regardless of your choice, keep one thing in mind: You cannot change everything at once. If you try to do this, you will fail . . . time and time again. Take your time. Determine what changes need to happen, and make small improvements, one at a time, until you have it mastered. Mastering a few tasks will be far more rewarding than simply knowing a little about everything.

As a salesperson, you work hard. You spend your days looking at numbers and trying to determine where your next prospective customer is coming from. You spend your time struggling to make those last few appointments count. If this sounds like the type of experience you are having, you may need to set down the pen, put down the phone, and walk away for a moment. You may be going about the process of selling, but you are selling the wrong thing.

Consider the person who walks into your office as a potential resident of your community. This person, or his or her loved one, is thinking, "Is this where I will be living?" or, "Is this place going to be a good place for my mom (dad, grandparent, etc.)?" Your job is to ease the person's fears and to show that living in your community is a good thing.

If you are like so many other people in today's senior housing market, you are struggling for the sale. You may have a number of prospective residents coming in, but you are not getting them to commit, and you are not closing the sale. This could be for a number of reasons, ranging from not having what the senior needs to being unable to match the prospect's demands in the community. Chances are, though, that the problem lies in the way you are approaching the senior and his or her family.

Look to the Future

Take a few minutes to look toward your future. What will you be doing in a year? Do you imagine yourself sitting behind that desk as you are today, talking to potential residents? What about your senior living community? What does its future look like from your vantage point? Will your occupancy be high? Will your finances be strong? Will you be pushing forward, or hanging back?

As you look into your future, let go of the concern. Of course you're worried – it's human nature to worry. You are unsure of what the future holds financially for your business and career, especially if you cannot improve the numbers.

It seems as if in every community I visit, I get asked the same question: "Mike, how can I shorten the sales cycle?" Well, I have some good news and some bad news. The bad news is that you cannot shorten the sales cycle. When you think about shortening the sales cycle, you are making it about you. You are focusing on *your* agenda. The good news is that once you implement the sales strategies and the not-so-sales-like mentality that you will learn in this book, your life will change, and your senior living community will flourish. If you are truly on the prospects' agenda and the questions you ask bring them to the resolution that they need to move in sooner rather than later, that will be because you truly care. The money signs in your eyes will have been replaced with eyes of compassion.

Things Have Changed

One of the things to take into consideration as you look toward the future is the ways in which this market has changed. Just ten years ago, selling in the senior housing market might have been easy. All it took was developing a community, and there were plenty of people willing to fill the rooms. That is because there were just a handful of communities at the time. It was easy to be a selective community; you could choose the people who would best fit into your community. The economy was booming and with it, the housing market. Today, this is no longer the case.

Now, within the space of a few miles, you will find several senior housing and medical communities. I was recently training for a client in Florida, and there must have been ten senior living communities within five miles of this client's community. The competition is fierce, and it is up to you to confront it head-on.

In addition, there is now less traffic coming into most communities. For a variety of reasons, people are staying home, at least until they can no longer manage it, or living with their kids, rather than moving into senior living communities.

What is one of the most common objections we hear? "We have to sell our home before we can make the move." In some cases, that is true. However, we conducted a study and found that although this objection is commonly used, it is rarely the truth. Hold onto that thought, though. We will talk about it later.

There are fewer people moving in, and fewer people coming in for appointments. Each one of these people, then, must count. Further, you are splitting the limited traffic that is coming in with all of the other competitors in your area.

Another concern is attrition. Across the board, senior living communities are seeing higher numbers in this area, too. If you do manage to move five people in, you lose seven. This makes for a complicated scenario when it comes to managing your numbers.

There is some good news, though. Most experts believe that as soon as the economy begins to improve, seniors will once again be looking for senior living communities to call home. The problem right now is, to some degree, the lack of funds. Nevertheless, your business, if it is like most others, can't wait until the economy gets better to turn a profit. You need people moving in . . . now.

The Baby Boomer Generation

Before moving on, it is important to talk a bit about your newest residents, the baby boomer generation. The buying habits of this generation are very different from those of previous generations. As you take into consideration your marketing strategy for Baby Boomers, it is necessary to understand this.

Who are they? These are the people who were born in 1946 through 1964 . . . and they are 77 million people strong. The first wave of this generation will begin moving into the senior housing industry in the coming years. With that comes a whole new set of values and concerns. This first wave of Baby Boomers accounts for some 37 million people, born between 1946 and1955. This generation, now approaching senior status, are among the people your community will want to target.

The Baby Boomer generation is different from any generation before them. They have very different world views. They also control most of the wealth in the United States right now. Their needs are different from those of earlier generations, and the way they buy is also different. Growing up in the 1960s changed the way many people looked at the world. The values of this generation came to be more focused on individuality and a sense of self. Here is a short list of values that this generation regards more highly than others:

- Relevance
- Questioning
- Enthusiasm for new causes
- Instant remedies
- Acceptance
- Flexibility
- Lack of Commitment
- Participation

Most Baby Boomers have a high level of expectation. They value being non-traditional. They are driven. They value autonomy. When considering the right sales message for this group, it is critical to look at their core values and to make changes to accommodate them.

The Baby Boomer generation is one that lacks commitment and needs to question everything. Because of this, in your sales pitch, you need to ensure that they conclude that your community is clearly the best one for them.

Baby Boomers have high expectations. Is your current sales pitch showing potential residents the value to meet those expectations? This generation is very focused on self, and finding instant remedies. Does your sales approach emphasize specific ways in which the potential resident will benefit from choosing your senior living community? What instant remedies does your sales pitch offer them? How does it solve the resident's immediate problem?

These are just a few of the factors you must take into consideration when selling to the new generation of seniors. Your sales approach needs to focus specifically on meeting the needs of a new generation. This is not an easy task.

A Word to the Leaders

I am going to repeat the sentence above. Most experts believe that as soon as the economy begins to improve, seniors will once again be looking for senior living communities to call home. We have taken this projection and used it as a crutch. Managers, you are letting your salespeople off the hook every time they play the economy card. I get so tired of hearing this excuse. I have not walked into a single community or conducted a single training session where I have not heard something about the economy affecting the demographic. I finally conducted an in-depth research project to find out the truth. In Chapter 1, we will talk about some of those results. The bottom line is that the experts are probably correct. However, if you continue to use the economy as an excuse and depend on the future to bring prosperity, it will not matter who you have on your sales team. You will continue to struggle.

I have some clients whose occupancy is at one hundred percent with a waiting list. I have some clients who think the world is coming to an end if they drop below ninety-three percent occupancy. When that happens, I get a call that sounds something like this: "Mike, we are at ninety-two percent. We had the momentum and things were going so well. I am not sure what happened, but I need you to come and fix it."

Some of you are probably thinking to yourselves, "What I would not do to have ninety-two percent occupancy. I would be the master of my domain. My boss would think I walk on water." Well, here is the bitter truth: If you wanted to be at ninety-two percent occupancy, you would be there. If you wanted to be at one hundred percent occupancy, you would be there. I will tell you what one of my friends told me a couple of years ago: you are exactly where you want to be in your life and business.

The majority of you are not buying this. That's okay. Over the years, I have learned to not take it personally. I have lowered my expectations, but I will not take on a new client who has salespeople who are not willing to be coached and trained. I refuse to waste my time and a client's money on salespeople who are merely going through the motions.

Leaders, start holding your people responsible. From top to bottom, the entire staff needs to be held accountable. Provide your staff with the resources they need to succeed. Invest in your team, but make sure you have the right players. Ensure that you have the coach who is going to take you to the big game. If you are not getting results, find out why and fix it. The longer you wait to fix a problem, the more money you will lose.

The bottom line is that we have a real leadership issue in this industry. When I say leadership, I am not referring to just those individuals at the CEO, CFO, CMO, SVP, VP, etc. level. A title does not make a leader. It describes a person's official function and role in the organization. Most people confuse managers with leaders. We have a ton of managers in the industry, but few leaders. The great news is that anyone can be a leader. When you have a person on your team who is both a manager and leader, you are fortunate, and you will see results.

Last year, I sat down with the owner and CEO of a very successful company. As with many of you, his numbers had begun to turn south. We finally got our calendars aligned and met for lunch. He did not know it, but I came to the meeting feeling generally frustrated. I was sick and tired of talking to people who want to complain about their situation, yet do not want to invest in resources that would resolve their issues. But this meeting rejuvenated me. This is what he said to me: "Mike, I would not say we are struggling, but we are certainly not where we were a few years ago. We were going through our annual budget and trying to make cuts, just like everyone else. Then I had an epiphany. Everyone else is cutting training and staff development out of their budgets. That is always the first thing to go. Why not invest where others are not?"

Finally, someone gets it, I thought. I know there are others out there who get it too. Some are my current clients. Some work with other companies that provide the same type of services I do. To those who are doing nothing, I have three words for you: *Stop . . . Doing . . . Nothing!* Do something . . . anything. Then make sure the something you are doing is the right something, and if it is not, try something else. Find a solution that works for you. And don't go with the least expensive product and services. Yes, sometimes you will find a good deal, but most of the time, you get what you pay for.

Leaders, it is time to step up. I will tell you what I tell salespeople during training and coaching sessions: to be successful, you have to do what others are not willing to do. There is no need to recreate the wheel. Take a look around you at the successful companies. If they are doing it, maybe you should too. If they are not doing it, maybe you should still do it. The bottom line is what Nike has been telling us for years – "Just Do It."

You Know All That

The information provided thus far in this book is nothing you do not already know. Some of the information in the remainder of the book will be familiar as well. Last year, I was training some regional managers at a very successful organization. The senior vice-president of sales and marketing is one of the most talented professionals I have ever worked with. She was one of those leaders (yes, not just a manager, but a leader) who sent up the flag and started sounding the alarms when the occupancy in any of her communities dropped below ninety-three percent. At the completion of the one-day training, one of her regional managers gave me this feedback: "This was good training. We learned some new ideas. However, most of it we already know." I was so proud I could have hugged the SVP when she gave this response: "True. But how many of your salespeople are actually doing it?"

You are likely finding it challenging to turn sales fast enough to keep the business in the black and your commissions high. But how can you do precisely that?

Rather than selling the product, focus on communicating with the potential resident on an emotional level. Here are the things you need to keep in mind when making a presentation:

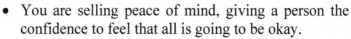

- You are selling peace of mind, giving a person the confidence to feel that all is going to be okay.
- You are selling social interaction. We are all social creatures, and you are offering the prospective resident the means to interact with other people with whom they will have much in common.
- You are selling security, the ability to feel safe.
- You are giving the potential resident and his or her family the validation that moving in is the right decision.

Instead of selling as you normally do, consider the emotional elements that pull at the triggers that compel people to act. Your prospects are looking for answers and help in making an important decision. While other factors such as pricing and location contribute to the decision-making process, it is the elements above that carry the most weight.

When you learn to sell in this manner, you are able to turn potential residents into long-term residents who are happy to stay in the community. That is what is going to improve your bottom line. Take every opportunity to create **Heartfelt** **Unexpected Gestures.** I refer to this as giving your customer a HUG.

The goal of this book is to provide you with the means to take your old selling methods and toss them out the window (along with those concerns about where you will be in the coming year.) You will learn how to make every single person who walks through your door matter to your business. Your senior living community will prosper when you incorporate these new sales methods, and you will prosper as an individual. You will have cared enough to help some- ✓ one. This is the greatest payment we can ever receive. The rest is just a bonus.

What You Will Learn

In this book, you will learn how to change the way you are currently selling. You will learn to focus on your clients, and to improve your approach to selling to make it more successful. You will learn to address the needs of potential residents. If you are like most of the salespeople I run across, you believe you already understand the concepts that will be explained in this book. Oh, how I wish we could all have an out-of-body experience and really see how we perform on the telephone and in-person. Well, here's the good news: although we cannot have an actual out-of-body experience, we can have the next best thing by implementing a mystery shopping program that will allow each salesperson on the team to see the presentation through the eyes of the customer. Later, we will discuss some mind-boggling information that has been discovered through mystery shopping and other research.

To achieve the desired results, you need to have a strong team, thriving residents, and a solid brand. You need to be at the top of your game and to use every lead to full advantage, so that even with fewer leads, your sales remain strong. The system we present will help you to accomplish this and much more. Rather than focusing on getting more traffic, you will learn to take better care of the traffic you have.

You will learn how to increase your revenues. You will learn how to improve the service you offer. You will add more to the community you care about. You will help people to understand what they want and how you will provide it for them.

Realize that people are calling on you in their time of need. Use your experience and know-how, the brand you stand behind, and the services you offer that will benefit them, and present the package in a way that shows this generation that they can have it all.

No matter which position you play on the senior living community team, whether executive director or sales counselor or regional VIP, you must understand this sales approach and provide the necessary leadership if you hope to improve the bottom line. This book and our coaching will help you through this process. You will have to be open to change, and yes, it will require you to step outside your comfort zone. You will not always succeed the first time you try something new. But you will learn to embrace your failures, because you cannot be successful until you learn how to fail.

You will learn the techniques to help you sell differently from your competitors. This is a must! If you sell the same way as everyone else, you are expecting the prospect to make a buying decision based primarily on logic – who has the most amenities for the best price. But you will come to realize that nearly everyone buys from emotion, and most of the time, that emotion comes from a subconscious place. We want the prospect's emotions to come to the surface and to influence the decision to buy. The primary motivation for the decision will be emotional, with factual and logical support. To accomplish this, we must sell first to the emotions. It is not as difficult as it sounds. We make it difficult because it requires a change.

Are you ready to stop selling and start caring?

Chapter 1

Can You Handle the Truth?

> *What concerns me is not the way things are, but the way*
> *people think things are.* ~Epictetus

"You can't handle the truth!" When I hear that line, I immediately think of the movie *A Few Good Men* starring Tom Cruise as Lt. Daniel Kaffee and Jack Nicholson as Col. Nathan Jessep. Tom Cruise is the government prosecutor attempting to get the truth behind the Code Red order – an order that took the life of a marine by fellow marines. Col. Jessep sidesteps all of Lt. Kaffee's questions with ridicule and sarcasm. Eventually, Kaffee pushes the right buttons and Jessep delivers his proud and most memorable lines of the movie after Kaffee proclaims he is entitled to the truth and wants the truth. Here is Jessep's reply:

> *"Son, we live in a world that has walls, and those walls have to be guarded by men with guns. Who's gonna' do it? You? You, Lt. Weinburg? I have a greater responsibility than you could possibly fathom. You weep for Santiago, and you curse the marines. You have that luxury. You have the luxury of not knowing what I know – that Santiago's death, while tragic, probably saved lives. And my existence, while grotesque and incomprehensible to you, saves lives. You don't want the truth because deep down in places you don't talk about at parties, you want me on that wall, you need me on that wall. We use words like honor, code, loyalty. We use these words as the backbone of a life spent defending something. You use them as a punch line. I have neither the time nor the inclination to explain myself to a man who rises and sleeps under the blanket of the very freedom that I provide, and then questions the manner in which I provide it. I would rather you just said thank you, and went on your way, Otherwise, I suggest you pick up a weapon, and stand a post. Either way, I don't give a damn what you think you are entitled to."*

So, what do I find so intriguing about this speech? When it comes to knowing the truth about our communities, many of us would rather not. It is more painful to know the truth and not do anything about it than not to know the truth at all. I normally take the role of Col. Jessep and will not spill my guts until I simply cannot contain myself any longer. However, although the truth that I am going to provide is not threatening to other lives or our national defense, they are truths that affect the bottom line in many organizations. Most people prefer to focus on the deals they are closing (incoming revenue), as opposed to the deals they are losing (lost revenue). It is human nature to want to feel the joy of victory over the pain of loss. Here is the bottom line: the main thing keeping your community/company from being more successful is not the low number of closed deals, but the number of lost deals!

This is a tough pill to swallow. Most managers have a fear of losing their jobs if they were to bring those numbers to the weekly sales meeting. So, instead of focusing on the facts and discovering ways to reduce the lost deals, we discuss the deals we have closed. Allow me to discuss some of those truths that we would rather sweep under the rug and never discuss.

Eighty percent of deals are lost over the phone. We conducted a Lost Leads study a couple of years ago, and this was a mind-boggling fact. We called about 500 different prospects who had inquired on a particular community. This community was from a location with an average population and an average number of senior living communities in the area. We discovered that most prospects (prospective residents or family member) typically called eight to ten communities to gather information. Guess how many they actually visited? Most visited only two or three communities. I am continually surprised by the number of people in my seminars who already know this statistic, yet seem unmoved by it. The truth is that when the prospects get off the phone with you, they are not looking for a reason to come and visit you. They are looking for a reason to mark you off their list of ten possibilities! As a matter of fact, before they even dial your number, they are looking for a reason why your community should not make the short list.

Eighty percent of prospects eventually move into a senior living community. In the same Lost Lead study, we were also blown away by this statistic. So, when prospects say that they can't afford it, that they have to sell their home, that this is just not the right time, or that they just started looking, then they are not being completely honest. How dare they? The fact of the matter is that they are human. As humans, most of us would rather tell a white lie and not hurt someone's feelings than to be honest and be responsible for causing that pain. Here are the percentages of prospects that eventually moved into a senior living community:

> ➤ 1-3 months: 45% = 180 prospects
> ➤ 4-12 months: 35% = 140 prospects
> ➤ 12-24 months: 20% = 80 prospects

Wow! Eighty percent of these prospects made a decision to move into a community within twelve months of the initial inquiry, and your community was not their choice. What does this tell me? Most prospects have made up their mind when they walk out your doors that they do not want to live in your community. Ouch! So, no matter how much we follow up, most of them will be hard-pressed to change their minds. I am not saying we should not follow up. I am saying that we have to do something during that first visit to create a unique experience that they will not get from any other community. HUG (Heartfelt Unexpected Gesture) your prospect!

We rarely get the true objection. So many truths were revealed in this Lost Lead study! It was easy to stand up and give these facts in a seminar. It was even easier once the facts were substantiated. In the study, we asked those "no longer prospects but residents in another community" the reasons why they chose to live in the community they selected. Here were some of their reasons:

- Close to doctor/hospital/medical facility
- Close to church
- Amenities
- New community
- Gated community
- Near golf course
- Friends lived there
- Price

Are those the reasons that should be driving the decision? Are there any emotions behind those reasons? Absolutely not! But it is our fault, because we did not give them any other reasons why they should choose *our* community. It does not stop here. We took it a little bit further. We dug into the community database and found the reasons they chose *not* move into this particular community. The top three reasons were:

- Price
- Needed to sell their home
- Not ready; just looking

Sound familiar? When we called the prospects, we reminded them each of the objection they had initially given for not moving into this community. Here is how often the objection given to the sales agent was true:

- Price – 5%
- Needed to sell their home – 10%
- Not ready or just looking – 5%

When asked why they gave an objection other than the truth, here were a few of their responses:

- "I didn't want to hurt their feelings."
- "I knew they could not prove it."
- "I did not want them to keep bothering me."
- "It just didn't feel right."
- "It sounded like all of the other places we had visited."

Guess what? We are spending ninety to ninety-five percent of our time overcoming the wrong objection!

They just don't care. About six months ago, a gentleman who provides services to the senior living industry called me. He just wanted to introduce himself, and since we were not competitors, to see if I would be willing to refer his services. When he found out I was a sales trainer, he began to share a recent experience with me. He'd had to place his mother in an Alzheimer's home. It was extremely emotional for both him and his wife. As with those who had participated in our study, he had called ten to twelve communities, but visited only three or four. Do you know what his most painful experience was throughout this entire ordeal? Not one time (telephone or visit) did anyone ask him how he and his wife were handling this decision. He said, "Mike, it was as if they could not care less about what my wife and I were going through. I know the majority of the people in this industry are nice. But in your training, will you please pass along that they need to be sympathetic to the family members' feelings as well? They need to care about us, too."

This was another *wow* experience for me. When we conduct our recorded telephone mystery shops, rarely do I hear the salesperson ask about how the family members are doing or how they are handling this decision. I have visited countless numbers of communities and have shadowed salespeople who have never gone into this level of discovery. Now, in all my training sessions, at least half of the attendees say they ask these questions and do this kind of discovery with their prospects. I then proceed to challenge them. I tell them I will conduct a mystery shop. If I hear them conduct this kind of discovery, the mystery shop is free. However, if they fail to prove that they get to this level of rapport-building and discovery, they will have to pay my regular fee for the mystery shop. To this day, no one has taken me up on the offer.

Additionally, I have looked through community CRM databases, and I rarely find that information in the salesperson's notes. This is a huge piece of crucial information that would make it to the notes if discovered. So, am I saying that everyone lies? Not exactly. I am just saying that not everyone tells the whole truth.

I am not a psychologist, but if I had to guess why we do the things we do, I would say we are all too often motivated by fear. In a day and time when we are asked to do more with less, we fear that we can easily be replaced. If we are not meeting the company goals, they will find someone who will. This fear directly affects how we sell. We subconsciously move into an atmosphere of selling that revolves around meeting a quota, rather than around helping the prospect. We get so wrapped around the axle in trying to close the deal that we forget the main reason we are there in the first place. We all have good intentions. I have never been part of an industry that is nicer or cares more for their customers than the senior living industry. The problem is that nice is not good enough. If everyone is nice, then you have to be different in some other way. You may actually care, but that is your own perception of yourself. It is the prospect's perception that matters, and if the prospect doesn't think you care, it doesn't matter what *you* think.

The truth sometimes hurts. Heck, the truth hurts most of the time. Luckily, when faced with the dilemma of giving the entire truth or just a piece of the truth, we are usually not swearing under oath, under penalty of perjury. And as difficult as it is to tell the truth, it is even more challenging to act upon that truth. Each of us has to make that choice. Today I have the easier task – the task of telling the truth. Tomorrow, I will have to hear the truth, and will hopefully choose to act in a manner consistent with that truth. Col. Jessep told Lt. Kaffee the truth, even though he thought the lieutenant could not handle knowing it. As I travel on my life's journey, I hope the Col. Jesseps who cross my path tell me the truth because they know and believe I can handle it.

Chapter 2

Defining Professional Selling

> *It is far better to be exhausted from success than to be rested from failure.* ~Mary Kay Ash

What is your current approach to selling? If you are like ninety percent of the sales force out there, your focus is on the bottom line. You are seeing every person who walks through the door as a dollar sign. This is the biggest mistake you can make in selling to seniors.

Let's be clear about this. If you do not have a passion for seniors and you do not care if seniors get the worst product out there, this is not the industry for you. In short, you can stop reading this book and move on. Rather than focusing on dollar signs, you need to focus on the person.

The main idea you need to grasp is that you have to stop focusing specifically on closing deals and making money. This benefits only you. When you put passion, caring, and actual attention into the sales process, your bottom line will benefit. However, you need to care genuinely. If you do, the financial aspect of your business will take care of itself. So, let's focus on professional selling.

When considering the sales profession as it is, we should agree on a working definition of selling. The process of selling requires the right person at the right time with the right solution for the right price, and the ability to recognize the right time to confirm or close the sale. This process is not as easy as it appears on the surface, especially when it comes to the close. Recognize that the sale is a process that will change every time. Just as every prospect is a unique individual, every sale is a unique process.

Professional selling is a learning process. It is not something that you do the same way every time. Each time you sell, you grow and develop your selling approach. It is a cumulative process. Imagine the new baby. He cannot just get up and walk. He must first learn to sit up, then crawl, then stand, before he can walk.

You will need to have a healthy self-esteem. You will need to have a precise, proven system in place, as well. And perhaps most important, you need to exude confidence. The strategies you learn in this book will help to increase your confidence, teach you a system that works, and improve the entire selling process for you. The method we will use is called the P-Effect.

Before we move on to understanding what the P-Effect is, it is important that you understand and change your way of thinking by recognizing that:

- The economy is not your problem.
- If you are not willing to change the way you look at the sales process, you will never reach the ultimate goal.
- If you think you know all there is to know about sales, you are wrong.

I challenge you is to put aside the way you have been selling and to improve your outlook. *You are selling to real people!*

Marketing and Referrals: It's Not About the Traffic.

There is no doubt that you will need to spend money on marketing, but you will also want to focus on getting referrals. In fact, referrals are one of the best types of marketing out there. While it is important for you to use these and other marketing techniques (and we will discuss further options later in this book) it is also important to focus on how you use the traffic that your marketing efforts generate.

Referral channels are at least as important, if not more so, than the traditional marketing you are currently doing for your business. The senior living community is, in some respects, like a high school. There is often the feeling that "If so and so is happy at the community, then it would be a good choice for me, too." Or, you might hear, "I heard that at the community where Mary lives they offer all kinds of fun things to do." These are the types of positive remarks you want to hear about your community. You want people to be talking about your community in a positive manner, to encourage others to see living there as a pleasant experience.

When you develop referrals like this, you will have better traffic. Then once you get people in the door, you need to know how to use that traffic to achieve the success you desire.

It's Time to Get Dirty

The challenge here is to pull up your sleeves and get dirty. If you are a manager in a senior living community, you need to know how well your sales counselors are doing. You need to be working with them to evaluate the sales process they are using. You cannot just close the door and demand improved numbers each month.

If you are an executive director or administrator of a community, you need to pay close attention to the way your managers work. You must know how your team is performing.

Consider this stat: Only the top five percent of all sales professionals who sell senior housing services understand that selling is a process, a process that needs to be done in a precise order to be successful.

"It's the Way We Have Always Done It!"

Here is a serious issue in the senior living industry, and it is becoming more and more prevalent. There is an amazing amount of turnover, especially on the sales and marketing side of the house. New people come in, and new people go out. We are looking for that perfect salesperson to help us increase our occupancy. The problem most of the time is not the sales staff. The problem is the leadership. Ouch! Now, if you can take that statement as constructive and not immediately go on the defensive, there is a lesson to learn.

We all know things have changed in the past few years. Everyone I speak to says we have to do things differently than we did before. Herein lies the problem. Those people who were in a sales role five to ten years ago are now managers, and they are training their staffs the way they were trained. They are passing along the same skills and techniques that were being used years ago. Why? I believe there are several reasons why they teach the same techniques:

- It is what they have always done.
- It allows them to stay in their comfort zone.
- It worked for them; it should work for their team.
- It would involve change, and change requires risk. (More comfort zone stuff.)
- Managers are spread too thin. They do not have the time to invest in each of their salespeople.
- They are "shotgun blasting" their training and expecting everyone to grasp the concepts and run with them.

The list goes on and on. Some of you reading this book may be adding to the list on the side margin of the page. In all actuality, most of these can be sub-listed under the first bullet – it is what they have always done. Here is an illustration by Costas Markides that alludes to this common pitfall:

The experiment involved five monkeys, a cage, a banana, a ladder and, crucially, a water hose. The five monkeys would be locked in a cage, after which a banana was hung from the ceiling with, fortunately for the monkeys (or so it seemed...), a ladder placed right underneath it. Of course, immediately, one of the monkeys would race toward the ladder, intending to climb it and grab the banana. However, as soon as he would start to climb, the sadist (euphemistically called "scientist") would spray the monkey with ice-cold water. In addition, however, he would also spray the other four monkeys . . . . When a second monkey was about to climb the ladder, the sadist would, again, spray the monkey with ice-cold water, and apply the same treatment to its four fellow inmates; likewise for the third climber and, if they were particularly persistent (or dumb), the fourth one. Then they would have learned their lesson: they were not going to climb the ladder again – banana or no banana.

In order to gain further pleasure or, I guess, prolong the experiment, the sadist outside the cage would then replace one of the monkeys with a new one. As can be expected, the new guy would spot the banana, think "why don't these idiots go get it?" and start climbing the ladder. Then it got interesting: the other four monkeys, familiar with the cold-water treatment, would run toward the new guy – and beat him up. The new guy, unaware of the cold-water history, would get the message: no climbing up the ladder in this cage – banana or no banana. When the beast outside the cage would replace a second monkey with a new one, the events would repeat themselves, monkey runs toward the ladder; other monkeys beat him up; new monkey does not attempt to climb again. However, there was one notable detail: the first new monkey, who had never received the cold-water treatment himself (and didn't even know anything about it), would, with equal vigor and enthusiasm, join in the beating of the new guy on the block.

When the researcher replaced a third monkey, the same thing happened; likewise for the fourth until, eventually, all the monkeys had been replaced and none of the ones in the cage had any experience or knowledge of the cold-water treatment.

Then, a new monkey was introduced into the cage. It ran toward the ladder only to get beaten up by the others. Yet, this monkey turned around and asked "why do you beat me up when I try to get the banana?" The other four monkeys stopped, looked at each other slightly puzzled and finally shrugged their shoulders: "Don't know. But that's the way we do things around here."

Just so it is perfectly clear, I am not referring to anyone as a monkey. I thought this was a cute illustration to get the point across. Some of you probably loved the illustration and are planning to use it during your next meeting. Great! That means you are getting the point. However, getting the point is the easy part. Implementing the behavior is the challenge. You will face resistance by those above you and below you in the food chain.

As an industry, we must change, and we must change NOW! The old way of doing things is not working. If the old way is working in your organization, then I applaud you, and this particular part of the book may not apply to you. One word of advice though. When you see the slightest sign that change needs to occur, you had better do it PDQ (pretty darn quick) or you are going to be playing catch-up.

Some of the companies I have worked for are catching on and seeing drastic changes in their organizations. Others move from one concept to another and jump on the bandwagon of the most popular sales and marketing fads. Here it is, plain and simple: Invest in a system that fits into your new sales culture and then stick with the system. Some companies, and some individuals, will experience overnight success, while others may take a bit longer. Change requires patience. Don't beat the salesperson up for trying new things.

Now that you have the background information you need, we will move on to the powerful P-Effect. Yes, it is that good.

Who Is Your Competition?

Quickly – name four or five of your competitors. It should take you less than ten seconds to identify your competition. I am amazed by how many salespeople have to stop and think of even one or two of their competitors. Well, you probably rattled off the communities down the street or ones that are in close proximity to you that offer similar services and care levels. Did you mention any companies outside your industry . . . for example, restaurants, department stores, Internet service providers, automobile dealerships, travel companies, and so forth?

My guess is that these other companies probably did not even enter your mind. That's okay, because when it comes to purchasing a home in your community, the prospect is not going to visit the Ritz Carlton to compare amenities. But the type of experience they receive there will be compared with the experience they received at your community. Here is an example that shows what I mean by that. Just recently, my wife and I enjoyed fantastic service at our local Red Robin restaurant. The service was our main topic of conversation. We made sure to mention this to the manager as we were paying our bill.

Now, when we go to the Red Robin, we ask to be seated in the section where *our* server was working. We love this guy and tell all of our friends and family about him. Every time I leave Red Robin, I wonder why everyone who provides a service or product cannot give the same *WOW* service I get at Red Robin.

How many times have you hung up the phone or left an establishment feeling frustrated by the lack of service? It happens all the time. As a matter of fact, it has become the norm, and we have come to accept it. Customer service just is not what it used to be twenty years ago. You can use this to your advantage. You can set yourself apart from others, just by the service you provide and the way you treat the customer. Why shouldn't your customers receive the same treatment they would get from the Ritz Carlton or Nordstrom's?

So, what is going to set your community apart from your competitors? *You!* All other things being equal, you, the salesperson will be the X factor. People buy from people. When they walk out your doors, they need to be thinking, "Why can't all of our visits be like this one?" If you have completely "wowed" a prospective resident who for some legitimate reason is still not able to move into your community, you hope that person feels disappointed not to be able to call your community home. Then, and only then, will you know that you have done your job.

Chapter 3

P-Effect Selling to Seniors

> *People don't care how much you know until they know how much you care.* ~Theodore Roosevelt

Before going any further, stop and think about this: When people outside the sales industry think of salespeople, what images come to mind? They imagine someone who, like the stereotypic used car salesman, is:

- Sleazy
- Pushy
- Uncaring
- Anxious to make the sale at any cost.

If you stop and think about it, you probably think the same things about other salespeople. After all, that's why we salespeople give ourselves titles like Account Manager, Community Marketing Representative, Lifestyle Advisor, and so forth. So, knowing that most of us have a negative perception of other salespeople, how do *you* want to be described?

- Helpful
- Caring
- Knowledgeable
- Genuinely interested
- Honest

When people think of me in my sales role, that's how I want to be seen.

Here is the P-Effect definition of a salesperson: A person who uses **personal integrity** to **help** others identify their **needs** and find **personal solutions.**

Now that we have a working definition of a salesperson, let's talk about the sales process. One of the most important guidelines to follow is called the P-Effect. Let's break down what that means.

The "P" represents the word *Primo*, which comes from the Latin word *primus*, which means first or premier. Our goal is to transform the canned presentation you are using into a formal sales process; that sales process is *premier* because it is yours – you own it and it is unique to you. The catch is that to be a premier process, it has to be your own process. It needs to be unique to you, and one you feel comfortable using. A good way to describe just how personal this type of sales process needs to be is to compare it to the rifle and the soldier. The two are separate, but they function as a unit. The sales process you create needs to be part of who you are. When you use this process, you will be conducting customer-needs-focused selling. This is what we call the P-Effect, or Primo Effect.

Now, let us define what *effect* means. It means something that is brought about by a cause or an agent. It is the result –

something that you bring into existence, accomplish, or produce.

Keep in mind that the P-Effect is built on a foundation of rapport and trust. When you are presented with an opportunity, you must approach it with unwavering integrity. Take the word *sell* out of your mind, and focus on helping people find solutions to their problems and ways to meet their needs. When you use this method, you will immediately increase your opportunities for success.

- **P**repare (Plan)
- **R**apport
- **I**dentify Needs
- **M**anaged Presentation
- **O**vercome Objections and Close

When you follow this process every time you have the opportunity, you will see increased sales. Did you notice the first letter of each step of the sales process spells PRIMO?

Keep in mind that perfecting this process will require continuous training, coaching, and accountability. If you are not holding your people accountable, then you might as well not even start the process. Accountability is the key factor behind any successful program. Leaders must step up to the plate. View every experience as another opportunity to grow and learn.

Let's take a closer look at the steps in the process.

Preparation/Planning

Many of you probably would not start your day without preparing for it. You probably would not host a get-together without planning. If you are going on a vacation, the majority of you plan accordingly. Preparation is key to success, not only in daily life, but also in business. But most people drop the ball right here, thinking they can just wing it.

The five P's are a great way to remember this: Prior Planning Prevents Poor Performance. You may be tempted to skip this section, thinking that you know how to prepare, or making the mistake of believing that you no longer need to plan. After all, you have years of experience under your belt! But everyone needs to plan for every meeting, and not to expect to conduct each one like the last. A true sales warrior will start preparing well before the interaction with the customer begins. In fact, the preparation may start years before the actual meeting, in some cases. Learning preparation skills is a lifelong process. You should not expect to reach a point in your career where you have arrived and can stop learning and applying yourself. However, many of you *think* you are there. In the army, we used to call people like this ROAD (Retired On Active Duty) Warriors. They were still in the army, but were merely going through the motions. If you are in combat, the ROAD Warrior is the last person you want in the foxhole with you. In fact, you would rather have anyone in the foxhole other than a ROAD Warrior.

KASH, Not Cash

KASH stands for Knowledge, Attitude, Skills, and Habits. These are the areas you will work continuously toward if you want to become the sales warrior that you know you can be. While you should be *striving* for perfection through this process, realize that you are not going to *be* perfect. Even the best and the brightest are not perfect – but that does not mean that perfecting your abilities should not be your goal.

You are reading this book because you want to improve your bottom line, turn more customers, and have a successful business that does not keep you up at night. You can transform your senior living community into a place where you enjoy being, rather than one that causes anxiety, due to those dreaded numbers.

You need to know your strengths, and you need to know where your areas of opportunity lie. If you are a sales manager, you need to identify the strengths and weaknesses of each of your team members. Every person is different. As you train your team, you will want to be consistent with the group while giving individualized attention to the needs of each member.

Even the best athletes, the top performers on Wall Street, and the multimillion-dollar actors in Hollywood, who make more money in a month than most people make in a lifetime, continue to work on building and improving their craft. They do not stop when they become successful. The best of the best keep learning, developing, and growing. This is what keeps these superstars on top of their game.

Preparation Makes Sense

As you consider these factors, realize that preparation is something you develop over time. Although we are talking here about long-term improvements to your preparation skills and to your overall approach to sales, there is more to this process. Consider the short term changes as well. Every day, prepare yourself for whatever new prospects are on the other end of the line or walking through your door. How can you do this?

- Gather as much information as you can about the prospect, especially if it is a new potential resident.
- If you are following up, study the notes you took during your last meeting. Familiarize yourself with the prospect's concerns and needs before you call again.
- Avoid asking the same questions you already asked. Instead, strike up a new conversation. *Talk* to potential residents; don't sound as if you are reading a sales pitch. Remember who they are and interact with them.

Preparation makes for the best first impression. It makes you more confident, makes the potential resident more relaxed, and helps make every minute of the conversation count. If you are prepared, you greatly improve the odds that you will make the sale within the first five minutes of your call or meeting.

When making a follow-up call to someone who has toured the community and filled out your questionnaire, think about the person on the phone. Plan carefully by first reviewing your notes from the previous meeting. If you do not prepare, you may repeat questions you have already asked, leading the prospect to think, *This guy does not even remember me. I already answered this. This person knows nothing about me. I'm not important to him.* These are the last things you want your prospects thinking, but if you consider your own experiences, you probably have had thoughts like this over time: *Hello, this is me you are not talking to!*

Building Rapport, Credibility and Trust

Another area to study carefully is how to build rapport. Rapport is a relationship of mutual understanding or trust. Rapport building is the most important step of the sales process. Some trainers teach that the discovery and identifying needs take precedence over all else. Although I believe discovery is very important, if you do not gain the trust of the prospect, do you think he is really going to be honest about his needs? We are concerned about the emotional needs more than the physical.

Credibility is the reputation impacting one's ability to be believed. Most of us enter the sales process with zero credibility, unless you were a referral from a trusted source. Credibility comes in many different shapes and sizes. The personality of your prospect will determine how much credibility you will have to sell. The key is to be professional and really listen.

Trust is defined as the trait of believing in the honesty and reliability of others. For the most part, we give our trust away. It does not have to be earned. When we drive down the street, we trust the other drivers to stay in their lanes. We also trust the signals to change in a correct and safe manner. We trust restaurants to provide us with food fit for human consumption. Think about it. We give our trust away countless times a day without even thinking about it. However, when selling, trust must be earned.

Remember, a strong opening is more valuable than a hard close. So establishing that initial rapport gives you a strong start in building a relationship. Every aspect of your life revolves around the relationships you create for yourself, both professionally and privately. Recently, it seems to me that many sales people fail to build relationships with the various people they encounter every day in the community. They simply do not take the time necessary to develop relationships with the person who mops the floors or the woman who launders the bed sheets. This oversight leaves a bad taste in the mouth of the person who is not acknowledged.

Consider this: You have called on a business, perhaps another senior community or a business you hope to network with. You are told, "Thanks for your call, but we already have a company providing for us and we are happy with them."

You hang up the phone and think to yourself, *Really? Sure they do.*

Why is it so hard to believe that people can actually have relationships like this with the people in their professional environment? And, what would you do to have that type of relationships in your own professional life?

Every person with whom you come in contact is a potential relationship. Remember that woman washing laundry? You want her to recommend you to her friends, just as you want the prospective resident on the phone to trust you. You want the family coming in to talk about a place for Mom to believe you have integrity. To make this happen, you must build strong relationships, at work and wherever you encounter other people.

If the initial inquiry is by phone, it may be more difficult to build rapport than if it is in person. It's difficult, but it is possible. You can't see the other person's face or body language, which can limit your overall impression of the caller. You have the first minute of the call to learn what kind of person you are speaking to, and what that person needs. You have less time than that to make a good first impression.

The bottom line is this: No matter how credible you are, it means nothing unless the prospect trusts you. You will not gain the prospect's trust unless you first build rapport.

Do You Like Me? Check Yes Or No.

Is it bad to want people to like us when we are selling to them? Believe it or not, I have heard managers tell people they are not there to make friends, only to sell. If you have managers like that, fire them. If you are a manager like that, do us all a favor and find yourself a new line of work. Why wouldn't we want someone to like us? People want to buy from someone they know and trust. That sounds like a friend to me.

So, how do we get people to like us? Are there rules? Well, there are certainly some guidelines that we can use in business or in life:

- We like people who like us.
- We like people who are like us.
- We like people who can teach us without preaching at us.
- We like people who lift our spirits.
- We like people who pay attention to us.
- We like people who are approachable.
- We like people who are genuine.
- We like people whom we associate with positive feelings.

- We like people who are courteous.
- We like people whom we are familiar with.
- We like people who don't take themselves too seriously.
- We like people who are beautiful on the inside.

So, are you a likeable person?

In Dale Carnegie's *How to Win Friends and Influence People,* he speaks to six principles on how we connect with people.

Talk to people about the things they are interested in. Morning, noon, and after dinner, we are all interested in our own pursuits. If you want to connect with someone else, forget your interests and concentrate on those of the other person. We can make more friends in two months by being genuinely interested in other people than we can in two years of trying to get people interested in us.

How do you find topics that people will feel comfortable talking about?

Try to see things from their point of view. Carnegie's second principle is one that he considered among his most important secrets of success. It is that we must nurture the ability to understand and see things from the other person's point of view. And the first thing we have to do if we are to walk in someone else's moccasins is to take off our own and put them aside. Do you remember that old saw, "A man convinced against his will is of the same opinion still?"

What techniques can you use to help you see things from the other person's point of view?

To begin, you should genuinely like other people. How can you do this? How do you "learn" how to like others? First of all, show a genuine interest. You must have a good time meeting people if you want them to have a good time meeting you. We often think that the art of communicating is all about how we (you and I) say things. And it is true, to a degree. But probably more important is the silent messages we send that communicate whether we are really interested in a person.

As human beings, we have a tendency to dismiss people who are different from us. We miss a lot when we do that. Rather than clamming up when you meet people who seem dissimilar to you, search for the common ground. We all have shared experiences, shared interests, and shared dreams. Search for the connections – the bridges that will help you understand one another.

Smile. Studies have shown that people who smile tend to:

- Manage more effectively
- Teach others more effectively
- Sell more effectively
- Raise happier children

Not happy? Don't feel like smiling? Fake it till you make it. Remember the old song that goes, "Whistle a happy tune, whenever you feel afraid or alone." It works. Remember that nobody needs a smile as much as those who have none left to give.

Make them feel important. We all need to feel important, and we all need to have our self-esteem nourished. Use a person's name. Remembering names is an important part of good interpersonal communication skills. For most of us, the sweetest sound on earth is that of someone using our name correctly and positively. This skill alone will give you an edge in building relationships, and consequently in your career development.

Don't criticize others. We don't get people to do anything by criticizing them. We don't get lasting change; we just get resentment. B.F. Skinner, the world renowned psychologist, proved through a series of experiments that an animal rewarded for good behavior learns more rapidly and retains what it learns far more effectively than one that is punished for bad behavior. This applies to humans as well. Remember the saying, *We thirst for approval and we dread condemnation.*

The last thing Carnegie tells us is that the only way on earth to influence other people and get them to do what you want is to talk about what they want and show them how to get it. That's why we always have to think of the WIIFM (what's in it for me?) when we are trying to get people to do things our way. Help them see what's in it for them if they do what you ask them to do.

Empathize, Sympathize, or Relate

Most of us have heard the quote, "Lead, follow, or get the heck out of the way." This quote is what comes to mind when I think of the words empathize, sympathize, and relate. These words are action words. That means you must do them. "Empathize, sympathize, relate or get the heck out of the way."

Later on, we are going to discuss the correct way to question. The key to questioning though is to ask more questions about the answer. Peel back the layers and get to the emotional level. Then you can empathize, sympathize, or relate. Here are a few basic rules to follow when attempting to connect with your prospect:

1. Do not empathize unless you can. Empathy is a huge connector between humans. However, if you have not gone through a particular experience yourself, you cannot possibly understand how it feels. If the prospect is a cancer survivor and you have never been diagnosed with cancer, don't act like you know what they have or are currently going through. Just because someone close to you has been diagnosed with cancer, you still cannot possibly understand what that feels like unless you are the one actually faced with that disease. You do not "know how they feel." So, feel free to offer sympathy or even relate, but do not empathize.

2. Sympathy is a powerful connector as well. It also shows that you are human and do not have ice flowing through your veins. If your prospect shares personal challenges and trials, offer sympathy. If you have gone through those same challenges and trials, guess what? You have earned the right to offer empathy.

3. When all else fails, at a minimum, you must relate. Perhaps you have not personally experienced the same emotions that the prospect has, but there is a pretty good chance you have. You see, we are not trying to relate to the experience, but how the experience made them feel – the emotion behind the experience. However, if for some reason you cannot share that bond of experiencing like emotions, I can

almost guarantee that you have a resident in your community who has shared like emotions.

I need to reiterate the bottom line. It is not the actual experience you are trying to relate to. The key is to relate to the emotion. That will require you to be somewhat vulnerable as well, but it will be the key to building a relationship founded on trust.

Your Smile Does Matter

As we just mentioned, one of the most effective things you can do over the phone is to smile. Are you looking incredulous? Sure, the person on the line cannot see you, but he can *hear* that smile. A forced smile is easy to pick up on. The person you are talking to can hear it, and you know it. Consider this scenario: You pick up the phone and you call your wife. You know right away, from the way she answers the phone what type of mood she is in, right? Even if she is trying to act cheerful, you can tell that something is wrong, even though she hasn't said so. This happens with your prospective residents as well. So your telephone smile has to be genuine and sincere.

Another thing to consider is the way you dress. Again, the other person cannot see how you are dressed over the phone, but you should be dressed professionally. Why is this so important?

Studies have shown that many people act the way they are dressed. So, if you are dressed in professional attire, your demeanor will come across as professional. If you are at work in shorts and flip-flops, your demeanor will come across as sloppy. Which do you think is more likely to earn your prospect's trust?

In-Person Relationship Building

Smiling and meaning it over the phone is important and a must, but it is even more important during in-person interactions. While many senior living communities do conduct preliminary interviews over the phone, most of the time, decisions are made at the community. The good news is that you will have an easier time of building a relationship in person, but at the same time, it takes just one shifty look or off-the-mark comment to convince the family that your community is not the place they are looking for.

In most of the mystery shops we conduct, one of the areas where salespeople across the board do poorly is making a first impression and establishing rapport. Some do not even bother to get out of their chair and shake the hand of the person walking through the door. This is an automatic failure, and sets the scene for a lost sale.

If you do not stand up, greet the person, and offer a handshake, you are conveying, *I'm too busy to get to know you or to help you.* Perhaps you do shake hands, but you do so with fingertips only. This makes a bad impression, too. If you make these mistakes, the prospects will be looking for the first opportunity to leave, and most importantly, will not even notice your sales presentation.

It takes years to build a real relationship, but it takes only seconds to build initial rapport. By taking the time to build rapport with those who call you or stop in for a visit, you are taking the first step toward creating a relationship that may pay off for years to come. Once people start to trust you, they will begin to open up to you and to be honest with you, which is critical to the sales process.

Identifying Needs

You have the prospect in the door, sitting at your desk. Now what?

When you are building rapport with someone, you are performing one of the most important steps in the process, and setting the tone for the rest of the call or meeting. Now you face the biggest step in the process: identifying the needs of the person sitting in front of you.

Many people miss this step. They do not take it because they are concerned with comfort. It is often uncomfortable for the customer to open up and risk feeling vulnerable, a feeling the person may choose to avoid. The challenge for the salesperson is to get to the prospect's emotional side. It is rare that people will willingly share emotions with just anyone. Would you walk up to some guy on the street you do not know and instantly start communicating your feelings? Not likely!

Most salespeople are not willing to break this barrier. They are afraid that when they do, the person will knock them right on the floor. Do you head out on a first date and ask questions such as, "So, what happened in your last relationship that you felt the need to leave?" or "You went through divorce, huh? What was that like?" You would not answer these questions, and should not be asking them, either.

But with your prospective client, you are not on that first date any longer. You have already taken steps to build rapport. You have started building a relationship, and you are building trust in your integrity. A person who feels comfortable with you will be willing to share his or her needs and concerns, and when you understand a person's needs, you have discovered the prospective resident's hot buttons, the things you need to provide in order to close the sale.

Managed Presentation

In the managed presentation portion of the process, you deliver the customized presentation you have developed, based on the prospect's true needs. This is the area where most salespeople do the best, because they generally love to talk about the services their senior communities offer.

You know the information. You are confident in talking about it. But, wait a minute. Don't just go and pull up your britches thinking you have this section down pat. You most likely don't. The problem remains that about ninety-nine percent of the time, you deliver your presentation at the wrong time. And if you have not followed the P-Effect process, you probably have not discovered the *true* needs of the prospective resident or the family.

Many salespeople just deliver a feature driven speech, but making a sale is not all about the features of the community. It's about the *benefits.* This is not a show-and-tell opportunity for you, but rather a chance for you to show the prospects how you can meet their needs. Remember, features tell, benefits sell.

The difference is in the presentation. To turn more prospects into residents, you need to use a *managed presentation.* This presentation is only delivered once you have gone through the first steps in the P-Effect model:

- Prepare
- Build Rapport
- Identify Needs

Once these three steps have been completed successfully, only then will you be ready to deliver a managed presentation. Here's what you may be doing: You greet the person coming through your door (hopefully with a firm handshake!). You learn from the customer that he or she is looking for a place for Mom. You ask more about Mom and her situation. You take the prospect on a tour of the community, pointing out all the great amenities it has to offer.

The main problem here is that you haven't built rapport with the person in front of you – whether it is the prospective resident or a family member. You probably walk through this tour exactly as you've done every other time, with a memorized speech. You follow the same path. *There is nothing personal, customized, or managed about this presentation!*

This is not going to provide you with the results you want. You have to be different. You have to pay attention to the prospect's needs (both physical and emotional), concerns, and wants. You will include these in your presentation so as to be able to demonstrate the benefits of choosing you and the things your community has to offer over what the next guy down the street has to show. And there is always a next guy. Always!

Overcoming Objections and Closing

Overcoming objections and closing is another step in the P-Effect process. If you have worked through each of the other steps, you have already accomplished the hardest parts of the process, and you will find that closing is easy.

Objections are not something to see in a negative light. They are a good thing. Objections simply mean you did not furnish all of the information that the prospect wants and needs to have to decide in favor of the sale. This is your opportunity to provide exactly that. Welcome objections, because if you do not get any objections, you are not selling and they are not buying. Objections are like children in the house. If you don't hear them, you need to go looking, because something is wrong.

Before we get into discussing the close, it is important that we define it. When I ask for a definition of the close in my training, I usually get one of these typical responses: *It's the check. It's the move-in. It's the final goal we are trying to achieve.* But the *true* definition of the close is that it is *the next logical step in the selling process.* So, the close could be a follow-up visit. The close could also be scheduling another time to talk. It could be a variety of things.

You must ask for the close. You simply cannot do business without being willing to do this. But first, you need to earn the right to ask for the close. To earn that right, you have to go through the P-Effect properly. This will increase your closing ratios. However, if you have not properly executed the P-Effect, you should still ask for the close. Let me say that again: *Regardless of whether you think you have or have not earned the right to ask for the close, ask anyway.* Your competitors are probably approaching the sales process the same way you are, and *they* are asking for the close.

In some sales models, you may be told to use a number scale to "test the temperature." I like using this question to gauge the prospect's interest level: "On a scale of one to ten, with ten being the highest, what's your level of interest in our community right now?"

This question works because the answer gives you the opportunity to probe and uncover possible objections. If the answer is anything but a ten, proceed with the following question: "What can I do to make it a ten?"

Objections – Real or Smokescreen?

If you have not been given any objections up to this point, buckle your seatbelt. They are coming. But will they be real objections or a smokescreen? Here is a very simple yet powerful technique to determine the validity of an objection. It does not matter what the objection is; use this technique whether you think you can overcome the objection or not. Let's say the prospect said the price was just not going to work. Ask for clarification. Ask, "What do you mean the price is not going to work for you?" Some of you are saying that is the dumbest question you have ever heard. Of course it means that the community is too expensive and they cannot afford it. Well, that's what you think it means. But asking this question allows you to drill down a little bit more, and you may discover that it is not so clear cut. Many of you will be uncomfortable asking what you perceive to be a dumb question, or you will assume you know what they mean and let it go at that, and you simply will not stretch your comfort zone and ask. Fine. That is certainly your prerogative, if you want to let the opportunity pass you by to determine if the objection is an honest one. Here is the million dollar question:

> "Suppose we could figure out a way to make the price work for you, is there any other reason why you would not move into our community?"

If the answer is yes, then it is a smokescreen. You need to do more discovery to find out the real objection.

If the answer is no, then it is real. Now you need to handle the objection. Here is the bottom line: ***Stop overcoming the wrong objection!***

Here is an easy formula to help you remember how to overcome any objection. It's called the AHA formula.

Anticipate the Objection
+
Handle the Objection
+
Ask for the Close
_____
=
Overcoming Objections

Chapter 4

The Big Picture

American business has just forgotten the importance of selling. ~Barry Goldwater

The foundation of the entire sales process is based on rapport and trust, which has to take hold in the very beginning. If you have a relationship based on trust, the rest of the process is much easier to tackle. So let's summarize the P-Effect sales process.

P – **Prior Planning** before each sales call.
R – **Rapport** with every prospect.
I – **Identify** needs that are important to the prospect.
M – **Managed Presentation** based on needs.
O – **Overcome Objections and Close.**

To make this even simpler to understand, let's look at the process as if it were a baseball diamond.

In baseball, you have to go around the bases in the correct order, or you are out. In the P-Effect sales process, the same rule applies. You have to go through the steps in order, or your sale may never happen. Now, if you don't go through the steps in order, will you sometimes close? Possibly. Most of you are not following a formal sales process anyway, although you may think you are, and you still close, at least sometimes. What the P-Effect will do is allow you to increase your closing ratio. As you begin to take small steps, you will see huge results. Let your results measure how well you are mastering the P-Effect. Remember, the goal is not to try to master everything at once. It's like eating an elephant – take small bites at a time.

In my training and coaching sessions, I am often asked how much time should be spent on each step of the sales process. My answer is that it depends. I know, it's not a very good answer, but it is the best one I can give. The amount of time you spend on each step will depend upon the behavior of the prospect. We'll go into behavior types more in-depth a little later. For now, I will provide you with a diagram that you can use as a general rule of thumb.

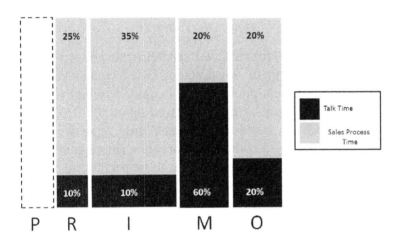

The gray boxes depict the percentage of time you spend on that particular step of the sales process. The black boxes depict the percentage of time you spend talking. For example, we are going to spend the majority of our time identifying needs, yet we are still only going to talk about ten percent of the time. How do we do that? By asking questions. More specifically, by asking open-ended questions.

The Redirect

If I were an instructor teaching this lesson plan, I would be foot-stomping my way through the entire lesson. The Redirect is one of the most powerful and successful techniques that I have ever taught. I wish I could take credit for it, but I learned from a fellow trainer. The Redirect has one sole purpose: to get you to the point where you can build rapport, in the beginning of the sales process. In other words, to get you to first base. If you are already skilled at building rapport, you may not need to use the Redirect very often. But research has shown that ninety-five percent of the reason we lose deals is the failure to build rapport. This is especially difficult when the initial inquiry is made over the phone.

Before we move forward, let me tell you about Connor. When I was living in Washington, DC, I was an assistant coach for a "coach-pitch" Little League baseball team of eight to ten year olds. Connor showed up on the first day of practice, and you could tell he was a little "special." Since we were not really a competitive program (more educational than anything), we allowed Connor to be part of the team. It did not take us long to fall in love with Connor. He always wore his hat a little cockeyed, and he had the biggest ear-to-ear smile I had ever seen. There were only four teams in our league, so we ended up playing the same teams over and over again. We got to know the kids and parents on the other teams very well. It got to the point where we would cheer for the other team along with our own. It truly became an educational season.

The odd thing about Connor was that when he came up to bat, he would never swing at the ball. So, fast forward to the end of the season. It's the last game of the season. We have two outs with a man on first and second base. Guess who comes up to bat? That's right – Connor.

I was coaching third base and had told the runner on second base to run on anything. I called time out and walked to the plate to have a word with Connor. "Now look, Connor. This is the last inning and the last opportunity for you to get a hit. How about taking a crack at the ball?" Connor gets that huge smile on his face and says, "All right, coach." Here comes the pitch. Connor just watched it go by. Strike one!

I called time out again and went to home plate to have another talk with Connor. I told him the same thing. Here comes the second pitch. Connor watched the second one fly by. Strike Two!

Again, I call time out and walked to home plate. "Connor, turn around and look in the bleachers. Do you see Mom and Dad?" Connor nods. "Well, they don't care whether you get a hit or not. They just want to see you swing the bat. Honestly, that's all any of us want. Just take a swing." Connor replies with his big smile, "All right, coach."

Here comes the pitch. What do you think Connor does? Yes, of course, he takes a swing at the ball. The story would suck had he let it go by again. Well, not only did he take a swing, he made contact with the ball. You would have thought it was Game Seven of the World Series, bottom of the ninth inning, and Connor just put the game-winning homerun out of the park. Both sets of bleachers went nuts.

I turned around to see Connor's parents' reaction. Mom had her hands over her mouth like she was choking back tears. Dad was shouting and pointing toward first base. I was thrilled . . . until I turned back around. Darting down the third base line was Connor. The runner on second was also running toward third base. Connor slides into the bag about the same time as the other runner. Connor stands up with this look as if to say to the other runner, *What are you doing on my bag?* Then a huge smile spread across his face because he realized what he had done. He had his first hit. I did not realize how quiet the parents were until I heard the umpire yell, "Batter's out!" I looked down at Connor and said, "Connor, I am so proud of you. You mustered up the courage to swing at the ball for the first time, and you got a hit. Next season, when you get a hit, I want you to run to first base first." Connor looked up and smiled and said, "All right, coach."

So, what does this have to do with the Redirect? Here is a typical conversation that happens when a prospect calls in:

Salesperson: "Thanks for calling The Villages at Riverside, this is Mary. How can I help you?"

Prospect: "Hi Mary, I was calling to get some information on your community."

Salesperson: "That sounds great. Can I get your name please?"

Prospect: "Sure. My name is Connie."

Salesperson: "Connie, can I get your telephone number please?"

Prospect: "619-248-3610."

Salesperson: "Connie, can I get your address so I can send you a brochure?"

Sometimes you may get the address, and other times you will not. We will discuss this in a bit.

Salesperson: "Well, Connie, I am glad you called because we have some great specials going on this month. We have one bedroom, two bedroom, and three bedroom apartments. They range in size from . . . We have three meals a day. We have an indoor pool . . ." (The data dump continues.)

Some of you are going to disagree with me right now. However, I have thousands of recorded telephone mystery shops as proof. The point is not to go on the defensive, but to learn. So, what happened here? The prospect called in requesting information. What did we do? We threw up all over her shoes! The prospect took us straight to third base, and we clung to that base like we had just hit a triple. We all have that Connor inside of us, and it is a constant battle. The prospect wants us to go to third base, guarding against interacting on an emotional level, thus avoiding a situation that might make her feel vulnerable. So, she takes you to third base to keep you at arm's length.

So, I give you the same advice I gave Connor. Go to first base first. How? Redirect! Here is what a typical Redirect conversation might look like:

Salesperson: "Thanks for calling The Villages at Riverside, this is Mary. How can I help you?"

Prospect: "Hi Mary, I was calling to get some information on your community."

Salesperson: "That sounds great. May I get your name please?"

Prospect: "Sure. My name is Connie."

Salesperson: "Connie, I would be happy to provide you with some information on our community. Do you mind if I ask a question first?"

Prospect: "Not at all."

Salesperson: "What's your current situation?"

Here is what the Redirect did and why it is so effective. First you acknowledge that you've heard the prospect's request. You then ask permission to ask a question. Lastly, you ask a question that will take the prospect back to first base. As the prospect is telling you more about the situation that led to the call, you should be taking notes so you can ask more questions about the answer.

Let me share a little secret. It should be obvious, but for some reason it's not. If the person calling in is the adult child or a family member, then that is the person you need to build rapport with. There is a reason why this is the person initiating contact, even if another, often the parent of the person calling, will be making the final decision. The caller, however, will be deciding which communities make the short list of those that they will visit. Remember, they may call eight to ten communities, but they are going to narrow the list down to three or four that they will visit. So, even if they say they are going to come in for a tour or will call back to schedule, more often than not, they are brushing you off.

So, How Good Are You?

For the most part, we think we are pretty good at selling. If we compare ourselves to other salespeople, we think we are pretty good. Here's some information that may surprise you: in the United States, five percent of salespeople close eighty percent of the deals. You are not going to like what I am about to say, but I am going to say it anyway. It's the truth and you need to hear it. *You are probably not in that five percent.* Allow me to explain.

Every sales training session that I conduct, I ask the sales-people to rate themselves on how they perform certain sales skills over the phone and in person. I have them use a scale from 1 to 3 with 1 being the worst and 3 being the best. About ninety-five percent of the group, regardless of size, seem to rate themselves in similar fashion. Here is the breakdown:

TELEPHONE (Self Evaluation)	
Sales Skill	Score
Building Rapport (In the beginning of the sales process)	3
Questioning (Open-ended questions)	2.5
Listening	2
Presenting	3
Asking for the Close	2
Overcoming Objections	2

The foundation and core of selling at combat speed comes from the thousands of mystery shops we have conducted and the countless number of communities we have visited in the senior living industry. Our telephone mystery shops are recorded so as not to allow for the "he said she said" excuses. So, not only do you have the recorded telephone shop, you also have the written report, which actually tells you how the customer felt about the experience. After listening to thousands of shops and sitting through live telephone sales calls, here is how we rated the way the majority of salespeople actually perform over the phone:

TELEPHONE (Actual)	
Sales Skill	Score
Building Rapport (In the beginning of the sales process)	0.5
Questioning (Open-ended questions)	1.5
Listening	1
Presenting	0.5
Asking for the Close	1.5
Overcoming Objections	2.0

Here is an interesting point. If you define "presenting" as being able to accurately verbally portray your community, most of you would be a 10! However, when it comes to customizing a presentation that meets the prospect's needs, most of us do a poor job. Most of the time, we never find out the true needs, because we do such a poor job of building rapport. Yeah, I know it is difficult to build rapport over the phone. It's tough for everyone. But tough is not an excuse for failure.

Remember, most prospects call eight to ten communities to gather information. They only visit two to three communities. So, when they get off the phone, they are not looking for a reason to go and see you. They are looking for a reason to knock you off the list so they can narrow that list down. This is an emotional time for the prospect, whether it is the actual resident or the adult child. How do you think the prospect feels after the third or fourth call after hearing the same message over and over? Do you think yours is different? If so, stop reading right this second. Put the book down and go call two or three of your competitors and listen to their sales pitch. If you think your sales presentation is much different from theirs, I have a challenge for you: Call me, email me, fax me, or send me smoke signals. Whatever it takes, get in touch with our company. We will conduct a complimentary recorded telephone shop on you. If your call creates a different and unique experience from most of the others, you win. I will be able to add your name to the very short list of those who set themselves apart. However, if your call sounds similar to the average call, you will have to pay for the telephone shop. What do you have to lose? Even if you sound the same as others (which you probably will), you get the telephone shop, which is the most cost-effective tool in the world of sales. Rarely does anyone take this challenge. For those who do, I applaud you for your courage.

The majority of salespeople sound about the same. It is a stretch of their comfort zone to do something different, to go a step further and attempt to build rapport. You only have to talk to the prospect once today. The prospect, on the other hand, will be speaking to eight to ten salespeople. In all likelihood, they will end up with the feeling, *Hey, this is me you are not talking to.* We don't mean to sound that way. It is certainly not intentional (for most of us). Nevertheless, the perception is that we do not care. If we can't be genuinely concerned about the person we are speaking with, we might as well be on a car lot selling used cars.

Okay, so we sometimes get lucky and make the prospect's short list. The decision probably has nothing to do with us, but has more to do with our community's location – close to their relatives, doctors, church, and so forth. It ends up being a logic-based decision, because we haven't attempted to get below the surface to the emotional reasons that influence people's decisions. So, let's say the prospect actually shows up for a visit. Woohoo! Most salespeople think that if they can get them into the community, they can close them most of the time. However, as I have already indicated, this is not the case.

When asked to rate themselves during an in-person visit/tour, here is how the majority of salespeople rate themselves:

THE TOUR (Self Evaluation)	
Sales Skill	**Score**
Building Rapport (In the beginning of the sales process)	3
Questioning (Open-ended questions)	2.5
Listening	3
Presenting	3
Asking for the Close	3
Overcoming Objections	3

Not bad, huh? Not if you are comparing yourself to the average salesperson. Now, don't take me wrong. I am not saying you are a bad salesperson. On the contrary, most of you are average to good. The problem is that most of you are average to good. Yes, I am repeating myself and my editor may remove the repetition, but I do it for a reason. If most of us are just average to good, then what sets us apart? What is the difference between a good salesperson and a great salesperson?

A great salesperson does what the good salesperson will not do.

Just like the telephone rating, I also provide a rating of the tour/visit. The results of this rating are based on the numerous tours I have shadowed, along with written mystery shopping reports. I agree that we do much better in person than over the phone. However, as you can see from the table below, we still have quite a bit of work to do. As usual, our perception of ourselves is higher than that of our prospects.

THE TOUR (Actual)	
Sales Skill	**Score**
Building Rapport (In the beginning of the sales process)	2
Questioning (Open-ended questions)	1.5
Listening	1.5
Presenting	1.5
Asking for the Close	1.5
Overcoming Objections	2.5

In *Good to Great,* Jim Collins says, "Good is Great's worst enemy." Society has reached a point where we settle for mediocrity. We expect average, so we give average. We have lowered our expectations to the point that when we do get anything above average, we are pleasantly surprised. If I were to put average on a grading scale similar to what we had in school (A being the best and F being the worst), average would be a C. Some people are okay with a C. It's the norm. It's not good and it's not bad. My definition of average is *the best of the worst.* So, are you satisfied with being average or good, or are you looking to be great?

So, What's the Solution?

A trick question? There are a number of solutions, you say? Absolutely. The key to finding the right solution for any given sale lies in asking the right questions. Salespeople tend to ask very superficial questions. This often comes off more as an interrogation than an expression of concern. Do you really care about the prospect? If you do, the questions you ask should convey that concern.

Your questions cannot be rehearsed. You should have prepared several starter questions that help you transition through the sales process. However, once you ask that first question, you cannot possibly know what you are going to ask next, unless you simply do not care about the prospect's answer. Most of the time, salespeople ask a question and move right along as if they never heard the answer. Why? *Because they do not hear the answer.* They are thinking about what they are going to say next.

Try this on your next prospect. Ask a simple question. For example, "What do you like to do for fun?" or "What about your new home will be important to you?" When you get an answer, drill down and ask questions about the answer. After drilling just a few questions deep, your last question on that particular topic (for now) will be, "Why is that important to you?" or "Why do you care so much about _____?"

By drilling down and asking more questions, you are doing the following:

- Showing the prospect you are listening.
- Showing the prospect you are interested.
- Showing the prospect you genuinely care.

It does not matter if you actually have anything in common with your prospects or not. You don't have to be interested in the same things that interest them. You do have to care *why* they do the things they do for fun, or *why* certain features or benefits are important to them. When you find out the why, you get to the emotional level. People buy on emotions, so we need to sell to the emotions.

Be careful to not speed your way to the emotional level, though. Depending on the personalities of the prospects, getting there will be more difficult with some than others. Treat the questions as if you are walking through a minefield. Do not rush; carefully feel your way through. Here is a simple way to remember how to walk through the minefield:

> **Ask a question**
> **Prioritize the answers**
> **Clarify exactly what they mean**
> **Determine WHY it is important**
> **Relate**

Here is an example of how your current questions might go.

You: "So, what do you like to do for fun?"
Prospect: "Well, we like to play cards, read, and travel."
You: "How funny. I love to read too."
                                    <or>
"That's great, because so many of the residents who live in
      our community like to read as well."
                                    <or>
"Well, I am sure you are going to love our library then. It is
      fantastic!"
You: "So, are you looking for a one bedroom or a two
              bedroom?"
Prospect: "We are looking for a two bedroom."
You: "Our two bedrooms are so spacious. The master
              bedroom has a . . ."

There you go throwing up all over their shoes. Your community sounds like the last one they just visited and will sound just like the one they are going to visit next. If you

don't believe it, put the book down and go visit a couple of
your competitors.

Now, let's take a look and see how we could have tweaked
things just a little, producing totally different results.

You:	"So, when you are not looking for a new home, what do you like to do for fun?"
Prospect:	"Well, we like to play cards, read, and travel."
You:	"So, you like to play cards, read, and travel. It sounds like you stay busy. Which of those activities do you enjoy the most?"
Prospect:	"We really enjoy traveling the most."
You:	"So, when you say you enjoy traveling, what do you mean by that?"
Prospect:	"Well, we love to take spontaneous weekend trips."
You:	"Spontaneous weekend trips? I am not sure what you mean by that."
Prospect:	"We don't even plan where we are going. We just pack a small suitcase, hop in the car, and start driving. When we arrive at a place that looks interesting, we find a hotel or bed and breakfast and hang out for the weekend. It's so much fun!"
You:	"It does sound like fun. My husband and I should try that sometime when our lives slow down a bit. So, what is the best weekend trip you have taken?"
Prospect:	"Three years ago on Valentine's Day. . . ."
You:	"If you don't mind my asking, why are these weekend trips so important to you?"
Prospect:	"Well darling, because of something you just said. Like you, we never seemed to find time for just us two when the kids were younger. We

realized that even though we were together, we were still drifting apart. So, one day, we took the kids to my parents' home for the weekend, and off we went. Jim didn't tell me where we were going. He said it was a surprise. I later found out that he didn't even know where we were going. We drove for a couple hours and then I saw a sign for a bed and breakfast. I commented how nice it would be to go there sometime. The next thing I knew, we were pulling into the drive. We had a marvelous weekend and made a habit of doing the same thing at least two or three times a year. Our relationship is so much better now. Even though we both like to read, we do not find ourselves reading very often. Reading is something we did before we rediscovered each other."

You: "I can completely understand how life seems to get in the way of our relationships. We have some residents who travel for the exact same reasons. I can't wait to introduce you to the Mitchells and the Smiths. They love to take weekend trips and I'll bet they would be delighted to join you."

So, can you see the difference in the conversations? Okay, that's a rhetorical question. I know what you are thinking. *Mike, it's easy to create a fake conversation, but this is real life. You just can't have these kinds of conversations with our prospects.* Really? Why not? First of all, many of you have never tried. Second – and this one is going to hurt – you really don't care enough to ask these kinds of questions.

Here is my challenge to you: The next time you have a conversation with someone, try changing your questioning techniques to look more like the second example. Drill down and ask questions about their answers. You will be amazed by the results. Also, take the time to role play with your colleagues. Identify your starter questions and spend five or ten minutes every day role playing.

Work on developing a list of starter questions that you can use to help guide you through the sales process. These questions should be general enough that you could ask them to any prospect. Once you master the behavior types, you can create starter questions based on the actual personality type of the person you're talking to. Until then, keep the questions generally vague. Now, take several minutes to write down three or four starter questions you would feel comfortable asking in the very beginning of the sales process, to help you build rapport. Feel free to use my questions or modify them so you are comfortable asking them.

Starter Questions (Building Rapport)

1. Tell me what is important to your mom in the community she chooses?

2. What is important to you?

3. What do you do in a typical day?

4. _____

5. _____

6. _____

Chapter 5

Selling Over the Telephone

> *Half the battle is selling music, not singing it.*
> *It's the image, not what you sing.* ~Rod Stewart

Most of us love our telephones. Many of us have SmartPhones so we can always be connected. However, when it comes to professional life, many of us curse the day Alexander Graham Bell was born. We would prefer to keep all phone conversations to a minimum and deal with our prospects electronically. Guess what? It shows.

As part of the process of understanding the P-Effect and how to improve your sales, many sales managers will use mystery shops. Mystery shops provide an opportunity to see what is happening in the business through the eyes of the customer. As I've said before, the recorded telephone mystery shop is the most cost effective tool you have at your disposal to identify key coaching areas.

The Survey

The mystery shopping survey/questionnaire is far too often underappreciated. The technology we have available today is amazing, and many companies are implementing systems that allow them to record all incoming calls. These systems allow them to track and identify which marketing programs are the most effective. I love the technology and think it is a great invention. This technology, however, does not allow you to capture the customer experience. The mistake that most salespeople make is to cling to the perception that the call went well and the prospect is interested. In reality, the majority of our deals are lost over the phone. We need to understand how the customer feels – to truly see through the eyes of the customer. That's where the shopper reports come in. Although time consuming, it's easy enough to listen to a recorded call and determine the basics such as:

- How many times did phone ring before it was answered?
- How long was the caller on hold?
- Was the proper greeting used?
- Did the salesperson get the prospect's name and use it throughout the call?
- Was the prospect asked to come in for a tour?
- What percent of the time did the salesperson talk?

The average survey will have approximately forty to fifty of these basic questions that can be answered by listening to the recording. Although these questions are important and necessary to gather pertinent information, the real selling should happen at the emotional level. The mystery shopping survey provides feedback as to how the customer is feeling during the conversation. This greatly reduces guesswork and gives us more solid information than our own subjective assessments of our calls can do.

We have conducted thousands of recorded telephone mystery shops in the senior living industry for a number of different companies, including almost all of the top fifty senior living companies in the United States. We have either been hired directly by the companies to perform shops on their own communities, or our clients have asked us to shop their competitors, or both. One way or another, we have probably "reached out and touched" your community. We have researched other companies who provide mystery shopping in the senior living industry, and the results have been overwhelmingly consistent with what we have discovered: eighty percent of deals are lost over the phone. We will discuss this in depth a little later.

If the community has a dedicated receptionist or concierge answering the phone, about seventy-five percent of the time that person does not ask for the caller's name. For those who do ask for the name, only about ten percent ask for a telephone number to use in the event the call gets disconnected.

The average on-hold time is about thirty seconds, and that hold time is *not* the result of the receptionist passing along basic information to the salesperson.

On the average, it takes at least three attempts to reach a salesperson. We have had some take as many as twenty to thirty attempts! After about ten call attempts, the shopper normally quits, and we hire another shopper to continue. Even though our shoppers do not leave messages (most of the time), it amazes me that many of our clients are not concerned with these call attempts. Their response is that our shoppers do not leave messages, and many times our salespeople are on tours when the call comes in. But what if you get someone who, like me, does not like to leave messages? Some people may not want to leave their contact information because they do not want to be harassed. Furthermore, I have yet to walk into a community where the salespeople are so overwhelmed with tours and phone calls that they cannot be reached.

About fifty percent of prospects are asked to come in for a visit. Many times, this happens in the very beginning of the call. When it happens in the beginning, the salesperson is sending out the following message: *I don't have time to talk to you right now. Plus, it would be easier on me if I could actually show you instead of telling you about it.*

Ninety percent of the time, the salesperson does not attempt to overcome the objection if the person calling does not make an appointment, but offers to send a community brochure.

Ninety-five percent of the time there is not a next step scheduled.

I could go on with more statistics, but I think you get the message. Many of you do not believe this is happening in your community. Some of you simply do not want to know the truth. I know because I hear it all the time. If you have spoken to me or another company that offers mystery shopping services and have said your communities were in good shape and you were not in need of these kinds of services, you fall into the above category. I can't tell you how many times I have called a company and they report that their communities are full and have a waiting list. So, naturally, why would they pay for these services? Their salespeople are at the top of their game. Well, we will talk about that a little later, too. If you want the truth and can handle the truth, you will just have to wait. If you do not want to wait, pick up the phone and call one of your communities. Then call one of your competitors. If the results are different, then call me, and I will conduct a free mystery shop for you. However, if the results are what I said, you will have to pay for that shop. I have made this offer thousands of times, yet for some reason, no one seems to take me up on the offer. Hmmmmmmmm!

The Close

What is the close on the phone? Okay, if you are the typical salesperson, then your answer is that it is to get the prospect to come in for a visit. Of course, this is where we eventually want the close to be. But we really need to go through the steps of the sales process to determine what that close should be. In at least a third of the calls I listen to, the salesperson invites the prospect in for a tour within the first two minutes of the call. Now, you are thinking to yourself, *At least the salesperson is asking for the close.* Well, guess what the prospect is thinking. *I'm not important enough for this person to take time with me over the phone. I feel like I'm buying a car.*

Once we have gone through the process and know we have a solution for the prospect, only then is it time to ask the caller to come and visit your community. If you do not go through the process or at least attempt to build rapport, you have about a twenty percent chance that the prospective resident will actually come to visit your community. Am I starting to sound repetitive? I hope so! If you don't get this, you are leaving a lot of money on the table.

Resources

There are several resources that you should have readily available. You should have a list of starter questions, a list of common objections and how to overcome them, and an inquiry sheet of some type to capture the necessary information. Different trainers provide different styles of inquiry sheets, although most of them contain the same information. The inquiry sheet is not designed to be used as a script, but as a guide or roadmap to keep you on track. I was asked by a client to develop a Pre-Call Planning Form and a Post-Call Planning Form. These are very simple, but a great resource that helps the salesperson to stay on track. I would recommend creating your own forms as you begin to master different steps of the P-Effect. If you are in the process of working on mastering Rapport, have your form specific to that step.

Selling at Combat Speed
Pre-Call Planning Form

Date _____ Salesperson Name: _____

Prospect(s) Name: _____

Family Member Name: _____

Reason for Contact: _____

Needs prospect may have: _____

Rapport questions to ask (REDIRECT): _____
_____
_____
_____
_____

Discovery questions to ask: _____
_____
_____
_____
_____

Behavior Style: P-Effect Steps to Achieve:

| | 25% | 35% | 20% | 20% |
| P | R | I | M | O |

Benefits you can create for the prospect:
_____
_____

Primo

©2009 Primo Solutions, LLC

Selling at Combat Speed
Post-Call Planning Form

Did you:

Properly Plan	❑ Yes	❑ No	Identify Hot Buttons	❑ Yes	❑ No
Build Rapport	❑ Yes	❑ No	Summarize and Deliver a Managed Presentation	❑ Yes	❑ No
REDIRECT	❑ Yes	❑ No			
Discover the Current Situation	❑ Yes	❑ No	Overcome Objections	❑ Yes	❑ No
Discover Urgency	❑ Yes	❑ No	Ask for the Close	❑ Yes	❑ No

Prospects Behavior Style

❑ Director   ❑ Relater   ❑ Talker   ❑ Thinker

Did you adapt your behavior style to the prospect's? ❑ Yes ❑ No

Who are the real decision makers? _____

What are the needs the prospect mentioned? _____

What is the urgency? _____

Prospects degree of interest (1 lowest – 10 highest)?

1   2   3   4   5   6   7   8   9   10

What is the next step for the prospect?

❑ Tour   ❑ Home Visit   ❑ Other _____
❑ Lunch and Learn   ❑ Follow Up Call

What is my next follow up step? _____

When? _____

Primo

©2009 Primo Solutions, LLC

Chapter 6

Selling In-Person

> *Many a man thinks he is buying pleasure, when he is really selling himself to it.* ~Benjamin Franklin

This chapter covers the area where the majority of us are the most comfortable – the in-person tour or visit. We believe that if we can get prospects in the door, we can close them. It's easier to build rapport face to face, because we can see the body language. It's easier to ask for the close, because we can see the buying signals. It's easier to sell the community, because we can actually walk the prospect through it and show its amenities, as opposed to telling about them. Everything is easier, yet we are dropping the ball here as well.

If the prospect walks through the door, we know we've made the short list. There is a genuine interest, or the person would not be there. However, we gather the same information that the last community gathered and conduct basically the same tour. We do nothing to create a unique experience for the potential resident or family. We think because we are nice, we have automatically gained the person's trust and he will want to move into our community. Then we are amazed when he walks out and we cannot get him to return our calls.

It's all about the experience. Don't get me wrong, the amenities are important to the prospects. However, it is the hot buttons or the emotional drivers that influence decisions. If we don't mine for those emotional drivers, we are no different from any other community. Thirty percent of these prospects are going to move into a community within three months. How much of that thirty percent is your piece of the pie?

People want to buy from people they trust. When it comes down to it, the prospect is buying you – the salesperson. All things being equal, it will be the salesperson and the sales experience that will make the difference. Once again, I challenge you to visit your competitors and see what they are doing differently. The good news is that they are probably doing exactly the same thing as you. The bad news is that everyone is losing.

Is It That Easy?

If it's as easy as getting seniors in the door, then why are we not closing more? Many will say the answer is that we do not have enough leads. "If I can just get more leads, I can close more deals. The marketing program needs to be more effective." Hogwash! If I had a dollar for every time I heard these words come out of a salesperson's mouth, I could start planning my retirement right now. Selling is a numbers game. I get it. The more leads that come in the door, the more we are going to close. I agree completely. After all, what salesperson can't close more deals if given more leads? Ouch!

The Thrill of Victory or the Agony of Defeat?

It's the championship game. One team will win and the other will lose. The winning team will stay on the field and get the most publicity. The losing team will head to the locker room. One team will witness the thrill of victory, the other the agony of defeat. Which of these two emotions – thrill or agony – is more powerful? Which emotion will drive that team harder toward success? Most would say the thrill. They know what it feels like to be at the top – to be the best. However, I believe agony is a more powerful emotion.

Regardless of who is interviewed, the players on the losing team can hardly wait until the next season so they can have another run at victory. They can't wait for the two per day three to four hour practices. They can't wait to feel the everyday aches and pains that come with the job of being a professional athlete. More importantly, they can't wait to rid the taste of agony from their mouths. No matter how many victories you have, you never lose that bitter taste of defeat – the one you let get away.

As professional salespeople, we too often forget the bitter taste of defeat. When a prospect walks out our doors and into the doors of our competitor, it hurts. But, it only hurts for a short time. Unlike professional athletes, we do not have to wait several months to get back into the game. Another prospect walks through our doors that same day or a couple days later, and the last one is soon forgotten. The agony of defeat is gone, and we refocus on the thrill of victory.

As salespeople, we need to be held accountable – by ourselves and our companies. When I ask a client how a salesperson is doing, all I hear is the number of deals that person is closing. I *never* hear about the deals they are *losing*. Have you ever noticed that the difference between the two words closing and losing is the letter C? If we want a true analysis of our company, maybe we should start focusing on "C-losing" or as I like to say, "see–losing." Sure, it's painful. But just as we often remind our prospects of the pain they are feeling, we need to remind ourselves of our own pain. As companies, our biggest mistake is that we focus on the gains and not the losses. We look at the number of deals we have closed as opposed to the ones we have lost. We are constantly looking for the thrill, when it is the agony that will drive us to greater heights. You are probably thinking to yourself, *Mike has finally lost his mind.* Well, let's talk about it.

Suppose each prospect that walks through your door is worth about $25,000 a year (on average) to your company. We will assume that you have forty leads a month. On the average, you close four deals a month, giving you a ten percent closing ratio. With these numbers, the annual revenue you are bringing the company is $1.2 million for that single community! Wow! That is awesome. Can you feel the thrill of victory? Everyone is giving you high-fives and kudos for closing so many deals.

Now, let's talk about the agony of defeat. So, you closed four deals a month, but you left six deals on the table. Based on research we have done, three or four of those prospects are going to move somewhere within three months. But let's say two a month moved into your competitor's community. Doing some quick calculations, the company lost a potential of $600,000 in revenue this year.

Let's take this one step further, in case you are not feeling enough pain. Let's say that the use of marketing, community events, outreach, search engine optimization, and other marketing efforts drives the cost of each lead to $400. Now, if you think that is too much money to spend on a lead, you may be surprised to know that this dollar amount is well below the national average. But, I won't try to make you feel any worse because you are not spending enough on marketing. The bottom line is that you have invested about $192,000 to get forty leads a month. As it stands, $19,200 was money well spent, because you closed ten percent of those leads. The other $172,800 can be added to the $600,000 in lost revenue. You cost the company over $750,000 this year! Hello!

The salesperson tells the manager that if they could get forty new leads instead of twenty, they could get eight new residents instead of the four. It does not take a rocket scientist to do the calculations. Based on doubling the leads, we can double the move-ins. So, we invest more money in the leads. Now we spend $16,000.00 for forty new leads. Maybe they get eight move-ins from those leads, and maybe not. So, what's the point?

The point is that the salesperson's closing ratios have not moved. Based on these numbers, the closing ratio is still at ten percent, regardless of the number of leads. The number of closed deals is directly related to the number of incoming leads. I don't know about you, but I find that unacceptable. As managers, we are letting salespeople off the hook. We invest in the leads, yet we are not investing in the person. We can all go to bed and sleep at night because we are bringing in new residents, and the company, as a whole, is doing pretty well financially. The owners and senior executive team see the bottom number and are content. The glass is half full, right? But here is the problem: It is our human nature to want to experience pleasure over pain. However, every sales trainer in the world will tell you to uncover the prospect's pain and sell to that emotion. Yet, as business leaders, we tend to hide the painful stuff and focus on the "feel good" stuff. We focus on the glass being nearly half full, when it actually is more than half empty. As organizations, we may be bringing in enough revenue to stabilize our communities, and that is where we tend to focus. But if we shift our focus to the lost revenue and educate ourselves on how to overcome that lost resident ratio, we will very quickly discover that the distance from contentment to unimaginable success is not such a huge gap after all.

As a manager or leader, you have to reach the point where you say enough is enough. If every prospect that walks through your doors is treated exactly the same as every other – and ninety percent of the time, this is the case – then you are relying on the numbers to close the deal. You don't have salespeople – you have order takers. Nothing will change until you shift the focus from quantity to quality. This requires an investment in your staff. Train and develop your sales team, and uncover their true value and worth. It may be painful in the beginning, as change normally is. You need to uncover their weaknesses and train to them, and you need to discover their strengths and continue to refine them.

For you bottom-line-up-front people, shift your focus to what is being lost, as opposed to what is being gained. As the saying goes, don't just give your salesperson a fish, but teach him how to fish. More leads are great, but quality trumps quantity. Don't lose focus on the numbers, but make sure the spotlight is not so bright that the other "real truth" numbers fall into the shadows. The change may be painful at first, but as we have all told our children, one day you will thank us.

In the 2011 AFC Championship Game, the New York Jets were defeated by the Pittsburgh Steelers. When Rex Ryan, head coach of the Jets, was asked if he would change anything about this season, his response was, "I would not change anything about this entire season except for this game. We only played one half of the game. The Steelers played the entire game. If we had played the entire game, we would have won the AFC championship title and would be heading to the Super Bowl."

How many of us are only playing half the game? The New York Jets had to wait until the next year to get another shot at success. Fortunately for us, we get a shot every day. Although we may have good stats in some areas, it will take an in-depth analysis of our entire game plan to see where we are dropping the ball. We have to ask ourselves if we can handle the truth, the whole truth, and nothing but the truth.

If we start looking at the losses, we get a completely different perspective. As salespeople, we get paid commissions on the number of deals we close. What if we had to pay our company commissions based on the number of deals we lost? Ouch! Most of us would not work for that company. Instead of getting paid, most of us would owe the company.

Fortunately, that is not the way it is done. Nevertheless, as leaders in the organization, it will improve our bottom line if we stop focusing on the number of deals we are closing and consider the deals we are losing. It's inevitable that some people will not move into any given community in a given month. Nevertheless, many are ready to make a move, and we are losing them to our competitors. We have to ask ourselves if we are really doing that good a job, based on the number of deals we close. As salespeople, we need to hold ourselves accountable for the deals we don't close. We need to constantly learn from our mistakes, and we owe it to ourselves and our companies to remind ourselves of the ones that got away.

Remember that although the thrill of victory is exhilarating, it is the agony of defeat that drives us to higher achievement. Just as we try to find our prospect's pain, we need to constantly remind ourselves of that bitter taste of defeat. Most salespeople and organizations will choose to block out the bitter taste, and as a result will remain content with mediocrity. Those who sip from that bitter cup will excel and raise the bar to unparalleled heights.

If you have team members who roll around in the sheets of victory and forget about the ashes of defeat, trade them for professionals. If they are so wrapped around the axle about what they have achieved, as opposed to what they could have achieved, they are doing more harm than good. If you have team members who say, "I know it's a team effort, but give me the credit for . . ." replace them. You need team members at every level who are not okay with the deals they lost. This may seem harsh, but it is the ingredient that breeds winners. It's okay to sip from the cup of victory, but spend more time gulping from the cup of defeat.

What's the Answer?

Am I saying that we should wallow in despair over what we have lost or what could have been? Not really. If we did that, we would all live in a state of depression. That would be self-defeating and would not get us to our goal of closing more deals. The solution is to insist on accountability at all levels of the organization. Hold salespeople accountable for revenue-generating activities. Work on increasing the closing ratio, and the occupancy will take care of itself. Work on the quality of the leads, as opposed to the quantity.

Salespeople, why should your company invest more marketing dollars to bring in more leads, when your closing ratio never changes? Company, how can you expect the sales staff to increase their closing ratios when you invest so little money and time in them? Create an environment where everyone wins – sales staff, company, and above all, the residents who have chosen your community.

If you are spending an exorbitant amount of money on marketing, stop immediately. Don't wait until it is time to plan your next year's budget. Invest some of those marketing dollars in your salespeople. Conduct mystery shops to identify where they can improve, then train and coach to those needs. Hire a trainer/consultant to come in and work one-on-one with your salespeople, and hold the trainer accountable for their success.

That said, remember that a trainer can only do so much. If your salespeople are not receptive to the training and are not coachable, or if they are not being held accountable for improved performance by the manager, then you have an internal problem beyond the responsibility of a trainer. But if your staff is putting forth their best effort and embracing the training, and there is still no improvement in closing ratios, show the trainer the door.

How do you hold the trainer accountable? Simple. Ask the trainer to significantly reduce his daily training fee and work on a pay-for-performance fee structure. If the trainer makes a difference, the company makes money, and the trainer is paid a significant bonus. If the trainer does not make an impact within a specific time period, you fire him. You may lose the investment for his time, but it is far less than what you could have lost. I have yet to run across a trainer who cannot provide some benefit, even if it is very little. There are, however, some who will charge astronomical rates and barely make a dent.

Accountability down the line is one of the easier fixes we will discuss, but it is one of the most crucial. Leaders, hold your managers accountable. Managers, hold your sales team accountable. Salespeople, hold yourselves accountable. And if your company is not providing you the resources you need to succeed, find a company that will.

Chapter 7

Setting Goals to Prepare

> *You must have long term goals to keep you from being frustrated by short term failures.* ~Charles C. Noble

Everyone has challenges in life, both professionally and personally. It is in how we handle these challenges that defines who we are and what we are able to accomplish. If you see a challenge and push it aside, you are one type of person. On the other hand, if you see a challenge and then strive to overcome it, you are a completely different type of person . . . wouldn't you agree?

In the senior living community, we deal with challenges every day. Do whatever it takes to overcome your challenges. From the sales perspective, we can eliminate some of those challenges by improving on our goals. Setting goals enables us to continuously strive, working through the inevitable challenges along the way, to achieve the desired end.

Managers should work with salespeople to set goals for the company. Then, my advice to you salespeople is to set your personal goals just a little bit higher. Shoot for the moon, and if you fall short, you are still among the stars.

Choose goals that are in harmony with your core values. Consider what motivates you and others, and how that motivation can help you to achieve your goals.

Now, let's break this down.

Daily Destinations

Goal setting does not have to be a hard task that is filled with uncertainty. By some surveys, only about five percent of all people living in North America are committed to written goals. You should have concisely written goals, not just a to-do list. Once you have set your goals and committed them to writing, you need to think about the goals in terms of *how* you will achieve the desired results. This is not busywork for you. What actions must you take to get from where you are now to where you want to be? Get in the habit of specifying exactly the steps you will take to achieve your goal, and pursue it with intention and commitment.

Have you said these things in the past? "Goals do not work for me." "I have no idea what I want to be doing in five years." "Goals are just too hard and I'll just fail at them anyway. Why bother?" "I do not need goals. I am doing just fine."

Most people prefer a quick fix, and in today's culture it has become easier than ever to expect nothing but a fast answer. But to achieve true success, you need to work toward the long-term, harder-to-achieve goals that require a sustained commitment.

The Benefits of Setting Goals

If you take the time to understand the benefits of goals in your life, you will find numerous ways that they can improve who you are and what you offer. You can't move ahead in your daily life if you don't know where you are going. If you have no destination, how can you plan for today, tomorrow, or any other day? Goals give you that destination. You will need a map to get there.

You spend time planning your weekend, but have you thought further ahead? Do you plan your life? Once you put a path in place, you can make decisions that help you stay on that path until you arrive at your destination or goal. But be aware . . . if you are focused on the path of least resistance, you may regret the decisions you make.

How to Make SMART Goals

Learning to set goals for your personal life will roll over into your professional life as well. That is why the subject is included here. To make goal-setting easier and more successful, one approach stands out from the rest. It is the SMART approach to developing goals. Don't be fooled by its simplicity. If implemented properly, it works every time. Here's what the acronym means: Goals should be:

Specific	(Specify dates, numbers, and times.)
Measurable	(Define and quantify the desired results.)
Attainable	(Be realistic about the feasibility of achieving the desired end.)
Relevant	(Relate the goal to your core values.)
Timely	(Set realistic timeframes for reaching different goals.)

When you write your goals, ensure that you have included all of these five elements. Be realistic, and make the goals you set relevant to your environment and to your future. Don't allow your goals to be influenced by others. Take ownership. Your goals belong to you!

When you use the SMART approach, you articulate what you need to accomplish and how you will get there. Here is an example of a SMART goal: *I will save $1000 by January 25th, starting on November 2nd.*

This seems simple enough, and it provides specific information that makes this goal actionable.

- It states what the goal is (to save a specific amount of money).
- It states when the action required to achieve the goal will start.
- It is relevant to what you ultimately want to achieve (a specific amount of money).
- It sets a time limit for when the goal will be completed.

Always keep in mind the value of setting reachable goals that can be achieved within a realistic amount of time. There is little benefit to setting yourself up to fail. Goals do not have to be long term, either. Short-term goals can actually be better for those who are just starting to plan or make decisions about the future. Most people need to see results in order to continue to work toward a goal. If you set up a goal that is five years away, you will not see the results of that goal for a long time, and as a result, you will well end up losing sight of it. In order to achieve longer-term goals, you need to set up daily, weekly, and monthly goals. Goals should become a daily exercise for you. They are the stepping stones that lead you to the path of your larger goal, and the success you achieve when reaching each of these smaller goals will provide the positive reinforcement you need to keep you on the path toward the larger ones.

Here's a good way to look at it, from the viewpoint of Charles Noble. He said, "You must have long range goals to keep you from being frustrated by short range failures."

It is possible to have success without goals. This is called a fluke. In other words, it is not something to rely on or to expect to happen. In order to consistently achieve your goals, you need to aim specifically toward the daily, weekly, and monthly goals you set.

The True Value of Goal Setting

Because goals are so crucial to the way you will sell to the senior community, it is critical to understand this concept. Goals may not seem valuable to you right now, sitting there and waiting for the sales message to come through, but they can help you to structure what you do today so as to make tomorrow more successful. For this reason, consider the following benefits of goal setting:

- Goals set destinations, daily or otherwise.
- Goals help to clarify the purpose.
- Goals help to motivate you to take action and to perform actions.
- Goals help to deliver a sense of accomplishment for all involved.
- Goals help you to have a benchmark to gage your success.

- Goals help to validate you and note that you are successful.
- Goals will build up your self esteem.
- Goals will help you to have clear commitment throughout your life.

I highly encourage you to stress the importance of personal and professional goals using the SMART approach. You will get rid of barriers – including procrastination – that are stopping you from achieving the successes you could have.

Commitment Matters

Goals can only be as successful as the amount of time and effort you put into them. Erase from your mind the idea that you can choose not to do something once you have committed to it. Instead of walking away from the tasks you have promised to do, do them. Goals can help.

The key is to commit. Many people throughout their lives *say* they will do something or that they will try out this or that. This is not good enough. You need to commit to it, with all of your energy, attention, and skill. When you commit to a goal, you can be confident that you are going to achieve it, whether in the long term or the short. It is not an option.

Taking Goals to Work With You

Where do goals fit in the workplace? Throughout this book, you will learn important hands-on tools to help you to success in the senior living community where you work. If you do not have goals for both your personal life and your professional career, then you are not going to use the information in this book, and you are not going to apply the concepts presented here.

What are some useful goals for salespeople working in a senior living community? Here are some questions to consider that will help you get started:

- What goal can you set today that will help you to achieve a better prospective on your career and day-to-day tasks?
- What goal can you set for the next three months in terms of how many people you will interview?
- When you set any goal, what shorter term goals do you need to consider to make it happen? What do you need to do today to see results in three months?
- What can you commit to doing to improve your sales approach?
- What goals can you set to reduce missed opportunities?
- What goals can you put in place today that will improve communications between your team members and your back-up sales team?
- What goals can you put in place right now that will help you to target the level of customer service that callers experience. What about for people who visit onsite?
- What goals can you create that will help you to achieve the answer to the question, *Where will I be in five years?*

These ideas may or may not apply to your business as it stands right now. The key is to get you thinking. What goals can you set today that will lead to future, bigger goals to achieve down the road? Where are the areas of opportunity for you? Start to examine your values, wishes, and desires until you learn what you want to strive for. Then, and only then, can you start working to build a successful path forward.

Goals are a good start, but they are not everything you need in order to have a successful professional and personal life. They are, however, where you should dedicate some time right now. Jot down some things that you can achieve in the next day, week, month, or long term. Then, make sure you apply the SMART approach to those goals.

Let's break the process down even further by describing the different elements of a well-thought-out goal. A goal should be:

SPECIFIC
To be specific, a goal must clearly state **what** is to be achieved, by **whom**, **where,** and **when** it is to be achieved. You may want to add **why** the goal is important, to help keep you focused. Not all of these questions will apply to every goal, but it is important to ask all the questions so you can assess whether your goal is sufficiently specific.

MEASURABLE
Measurability applies to both the end result and the mile-stones along the way to attaining a goal. It answers the questions of quantity – how much, how often, how many? The milestones are signs along the way that will tell you that you are on the right track to achieving your goal. For instance, your ultimate goal may be to make $60,000 in a year, but the milestones may be to make $5,000 every month, which will add up to $60,000 in twelve months. By focusing on making $5,000 dollars every month, you will ultimately reach your goal of $60,000. This makes the goal

more attainable, because it is easier to think of ways to make $5,000 than to make $60,000.

It has been said that what cannot be measured cannot be managed. This is often true when it comes to goals. Sometimes it is difficult to measure a goal, but you can usually find an indirect measurement that applies.

ATTAINABLE

You should ensure that the goals you set are achievable. Firstly, you must believe that you can manage to do what you are setting out to do. If you set goals that are unbelievable even to yourself, it is very unlikely that you will achieve them.

This is equally important when setting goals for a group, or in a corporate setting. If the people for whom the goals are being set do not believe they can attain them, it is unlikely they will work wholeheartedly toward achieving those goals. Agreement and participation in the SMART goal-setting process is important to ensure that most of your staff recognize that the goals *are* realistic.

When deciding whether a goal is realistic or even possible, be careful that you do not limit yourself based on what other people believe is achievable. Set your own standards by understanding your own abilities, strengths, and weaknesses.

RELEVANT

Your goals must be relevant to what you want to achieve in both the short term and the long term. Understanding your organizational or personal vision, mission, and purpose is critical. Sometimes you may be tempted to do something because it appears easy and sounds great, only to discover later on that it has no long-term significance to what you want to achieve as an individual or an organization.

TIMELY
This sometimes overlaps with Specific, but it aims to ensure that you put a time frame to your goals. Someone once said that a goal is a dream with a time frame. Simply deciding by what point in time you want to achieve something can be a good motivator. It can prevent you from procrastinating, because you know that you are working toward a deadline.

"Failing to Plan is Planning to Fail"

If you find yourself unable to set a SMART goal, it is likely that your plans for the future are not clear enough, and you need to work on them. Don't be tempted to skip the process of SMART goal setting and "get on with it" without fully analyzing your goals. Doing this careful planning at the beginning will save you a lot of time and disappointment at a later stage, and you will avoid making costly mistakes. You can use the chart below as a guideline.

Goals					
INTEN-TION	SPECIFIC	MEASUR-ABLE	ATTAIN-ABLE	RELE-VANT	TIMELY
What is it you want to achieve?	Who? What? Why? Where? When?	How much? How often? How many?	Achievable?	Is it important to what you want to ulti-mately achieve?	When?

Phrasing your SMART Goals

In the spaces below, develop a statement defining your specific goals, incorporating as many of the elements that you worked on above as possible into the statement. This will include the actions you plan to take to meet this goal, your timeline, and how it will meet the organizational or personal goal you are addressing. Also indicate what types of additional skills and resources are necessary to facilitate this goal.

GOAL 1: _____

_____

_____

_____

GOAL 2: _____

_____

_____

_____

GOAL 3: _____

_____

_____

_____

GOAL 4: _____

_____

_____

_____

Chapter 8

Motivation Means Everything

> *Some of the world's greatest feats were accomplished by people not smart enough to know they were impossible.* ~Doug Larson

Motivation is important enough to have its own full chapter in this book. What you learn in this chapter will influence how well you do in your business, whether you realize this or not. If you are a sales manager in a senior living community, you are likely to be looking for a magic answer to the question, *What is going to get my counselors to turn the most sales?*

How do you feel when you wake up in the morning? Are you tired from overworking the night before? Do you dread getting up, showering, and heading off to the community center? Or do you find yourself excited about what the day holds? This is all about motivation. When you have the right level of motivation, you have the right attitude about selling.

All people are different in how they act, how they respond to situations, and how they interact with each other. We are all human, and that makes us unique. What motivates your team member may be different than what motivates you. One thing is clear though: we need motivation to change. Change is required to reach new heights of success. Motivation guides you through your personal and professional life. What motivates you?

Exploring Motivation

The problem is, no matter what managers do, there is very little that can motivate people outside of their own needs. Motivation comes from inside you. You are really the only source of your own motivation. Someone above you may be able to put some fire under you to make you start moving, but the only way to get from one point to the next is by being motivated from within.

When you are properly motivated, there is a better opportunity to understand and appreciate the relationship between your personal goals and your career goals. Although many feel that personal goals are more important and valuable, this is not always the case. In fact, if you are successful with your professional goals, you will often be better able to pursue your personal goals. Why is that? It's this thing called money. How else can you do the things you want to do, or save for your family's future?

Properly motivating yourself to achieve your professional goals will inevitably help you to make personal goals come to pass. This all comes from the attitude you apply to your work. Do you have to go to work, or do you choose to go to work?

Two Aspects of Motivation

As you consider the role motivation plays in life, you will need to understand the two ways in which people can be motivated. First, we can be motivated by the negative occurrences. And, we can be motivated by experiencing positive outcomes.

Stress and motivation are intimately intertwined. Positive and negative stress affect the outcome of your every day. I challenge you to take a closer look at the types of stress you face right now, today.

Also, consider that in the hierarchy of human needs, lower level or basic needs, including food, clothing, and shelter must be satisfied before the higher level needs can be achieved. If you have satisfied the lower level needs, and most of us have, then we can begin to think about the higher ones. But many times, when our basic needs have been satisfied, we become complacent. Fully satisfied needs don't motivate us; it is the unsatisfied ones that will spur us on. So we need to aim at the higher level needs that have yet to be satisfied and make them our goals. You can use SMART goals to stimulate your quest to reach the higher level human needs that add richness to life.

Focus on Values, Integrity, and Dignity

An important aspect of every life to keep in mind is personal values. Where do personal values come from? Your values develop over time. In many cases, they are formed early in life. Culture, religion, political viewpoints, and experiences all influence your value system. Since each person's past is different, each person's values will be different.

You have integrity if you uphold your personal values, even in the face of negative responses from others. Your personal values are related to your choices. Your values guide each of the decisions that you choose to make.

Integrity is an internal framework of principles and values that forms the basis for your actions. The principles you value and the degree to which you are willing to adhere to those principles will determine the actions that you take. The internal consistency of one's values will influence that person's actions, and will determine the person's level of integrity.

What is dignity? Dignity involves the expectation of personal respect or esteem. When we esteem persons or things, we give them value. When we are esteemed by ourselves and others, we are living a life of dignity. We are all looking for some form of dignity in our lives. Dignity is not something that is given away, though. It must be earned. Regardless of our own perceptions, most of our prospects have earned their dignity and deserve to be treated accordingly.

Integrity is Often Lacking

Do people trust you? Are you loyal? Do you have integrity, which is manifested through sincerity, honesty, and candor? When you have integrity, you avoid deception. You choose the truth, and when you do, you stand your ground, even in the face of opposition. You do not tell those little white lies. You make commitments and you keep them. You are responsible. You are the type of person who asks, *How can I improve?*

Do you exercise integrity? Be honest with yourself and with those around you. Most people, but not all, can say they try. What does integrity actually do for you? If you try to exercise integrity consistently, your life will be more fulfilling. You will have a more joyful, powerful, and dignified life, and will earn the love and admiration of others.

If you display integrity, you inspire trust and respect. You help people to achieve peace of mind. Thus, you are the type of person who can succeed in the senior community sales business, because these qualities inspire the people who walk through the door as your prospective clients to believe in you and what you stand for. People trust you, and because they trust you, they want to work with you, and they want to live in the senior community you work for. They believe what you say. You do not have to prove yourself when your integrity shines through.

Explore Your Own Values

If you want to find success in this industry, you should take some time to look deep within yourself to examine your values and beliefs. Does what you see there coincide with what you project to others? People can easily see if you are trying to hide something, and if it appears that you are, you will appear untrustworthy. To be a successful sales warrior, you need to convey trustworthiness. *The only way to do this is to actually be a trustworthy person.*

Consider your own values right now. A value is defined as a belief, mission, or philosophy that is meaningful. You have a core set of personal values, even if you have not stopped to analyze what they are. Values are the things that are most important to you, closest to your heart. Your values guide your every decision, both personal and professional.

Your Business's Most Valuable Asset

Answer this question quickly: What is your most valuable business asset? You may be thinking about your balance sheet, but that is likely not the right answer. It is not the location of your community center, the features of the community, the accounts receivable, or the income generated by the business. Your most valuable asset is your customer list. This is the record of the people who make your business possible. If you are not treating your customer list as your business's most valuable asset, then your business is losing money and will be unable to stand for long.

The Hardest Sale

The hardest sale to make is the first one, when you sell yourself to your customers by making a favorable first impression. From that first interaction, you are going to either win or lose the customers' trust. If you earn their trust, you will be opening the door to more sales and more referrals.

Most businesses spend more money and time on bringing in new business than they do on anything else. The problem with this, though, is that you are neglecting clients you already have. And these clients are often your very best source of new business.

The Lifetime Value of a Customer

One of the most important concepts to understand is the lifetime value of a customer – that is, the value of a customer to your business over the long term. Rather than a onetime paycheck, the lifetime value of a customer extends over a longer period of time. When you understand this, you can see the value of placing assets, including time and money, into managing your relationship with each customer, long after the initial sale is closed.

In your business, are you mostly looking at the response ratio to your marketing – how many people respond to your marketing, relative to the number of messages delivered. If so, you could be misjudging the total effectiveness of your marketing. Instead of focusing only on the response ratio, look at the actual return on your investment, taking into consideration the lifetime value of the customer you gained as a result of the marketing campaign.

When you do this, you will see that you can spend more on promotions, as long as they produce long-term rewards for your business. When you look at the actual value of the customer over a lifetime, you will be able to see specific, significant business growth. Consider this: Once you know the value of a customer over the long term, it is easier to see the actual rewards to your business that the customer offers. Then, you can better see where your investment is going, and you may be willing to spend a bit more on a promotion that drives that customer to you. After all, your competitors are less likely to think this way!

Making Values Front and Center

Now let's take a step back and look again at P-Effect and its relationship to your personal values. Here is a written exercise that you can attempt when you find the time. Take the very first step toward changing your sales blueprint. Be conscious of how it has been programmed. Sit back and think; remember the things that you have heard from your colleagues, the things that you have seen when you go like a customer in another store, and the specific incidents that may have shaped your sales values. Fill in the following lines as you remember them. You are not required to write down everything within fifteen minutes; this is not a test. You may need days and weeks to remember a point worth noting. Jot it down for yourself and maintain it as a record. The idea is to be aware of how and why your values have been shaped in sales matters. Believe me, it will help you.

What did you hear and how did it affect the way you feel about your product?

1. _____

2. _____

3. _____

4. _____

5. _____

What did you see and how did it affect the way you feel about customers?

1. _____

2. _____

3. _____

4. _____

5. _____

What were the specific incidents that affected you and how did they affect the way you feel about quality service?

1. _____

2. _____

3. _____

4. _____

5. _____

When you do this, you are becoming more conscious of the things that are affecting you and your business. Take note of these things, and become aware of them. When you are conscious of the influences on your values, you can use this knowledge to influence your outcomes.

You may begin to realize that some of your values have been unduly influenced by others, when they should be coming from within yourself. You are a complete person. You do not need to live behind others. Your thoughts are not an extension of another person's thoughts, opinions, or words. You can work on changing values that have resulted from a negative influence, even those values transmitted to you from your parents when you were a child. It is important to make this break if you find that you are clinging to values that have no place in your life or business.

Once you have reprogrammed your value system, the next thing to do is to announce that you are a different person, committed to overcoming the negative thinking that is holding you back. You can now emerge as a new person in your own right, without excessive influence from others, but with your own original thoughts and opinions. Take the time to print an announcement of your new personhood. Place these printed sheets in areas where you will see them every day, throughout the day. This will give you the best possible opportunity to build within yourself a strong person.

What does this do to your ability to sell? A great deal! When the next prospect phones you or the next person walks through your door, you will exude self-confidence. A person who is confident in who he or she is from the inside out is one who can achieve any goal.

Take a deep breath. You have accomplished much in this chapter toward changing *you*. That is a big step toward achieving your goals.

Chapter 9

Behavior Styles and P-Effect: The Link

> *To be successful, a man must exert an effective influence upon his brothers and upon his associates, and the degree in which he accomplishes this depends on the personality of the man. The incandescence of which he is capable. The flame of fire that burns inside of him. The magnetism which draws the heart of other men to him.* ~Vince Lombardi

Does behavior matter? Does it matter who a person is, what kind of attitude he brings to the table, and how he sees his day? Yes, it does matter. It matters to that person's quality of life, and it also plays a role in your successful relationship with that person.

What does this have to do with P-Effect, the innovative system that preaches the importance of "warriorship" as the key attitude to boost your successful sales career? Recall the definition of a salesperson, associated with the P-Effect system, that we gave earlier: A salesperson is a person who uses personal integrity to help others identify their needs and find personal solutions.

Here's the link: To identify the needs of others requires a deeper level of understanding of behavior types and styles; therefore, in order to become a P-Effect sales warrior, the salesperson must learn a great deal about human behavior.

The Golden Rule

Do unto others as you would have them do unto you. In other words, treat others the way you want to be treated, right? Well, who am I to dispute the Bible? I certainly believe in the Golden Rule; there is a time and place in our lives for it. However, when it comes to selling and relationships, you need to consider another rule. It's called the Platinum Rule: *Treat others the way* they *want and need to be treated.*

Here is an example: I do not care for the details, so, I prefer that you give me the *Reader's Digest* version. My wife, Lisa, can be telling me about a five minute phone call, yet it will take her ten minutes to relate the details of the call. About one minute into the details, I have already checked out. She likes to call it selective listening. I agree. On the other hand, if I'm telling *her* about a five minute call, I can give her a description in about ten seconds. As a result, Lisa will ask an abundance of questions until she gets the detailed information she needs. If we were to abide by the Golden Rule, our communication would be terrible. Lisa would be frustrated because of the lack of details, and I would be frustrated over the excess of details. So, to keep peace in the home, we have to adopt the Platinum Rule. I need to make a conscious effort to provide more details, no matter how painful it is for me. Lisa has to make an effort to provide fewer details, no matter how tempted she is to keep going.

In the sales process, is it exactly the same. We need to be able to recognize the prospect's behavior type and adapt appropriately. If the prospect and salesperson have similar personalities, we can use the Golden Rule. However, if they have different personalities, the Platinum Rule applies. For example, you may be someone who loves to socialize. Your prospect may be more of an analytical person who is very detailed oriented. Although you would love to talk about the weather or what you did this weekend, the prospect wants the facts. This does not mean that you completely ignore the step of building rapport, although you will spend less time in this stage of the process.

Every person you interact with is going to be different from you in some way. People all have different values, and therefore they will make decisions differently than you do. Each of us communicates in unique ways, both verbally and nonverbally. Understanding behavior types is critical if you want to build your business and increase your sales. Learn to communicate by first understanding your own behavior type, then recognizing the behavior types of other people. Then, you can adapt the way you communicate with the person based on his or her behavior type.

If you are looking to create a unique selling experience, master the ability to discern and sell to the different behavior types. Just like everything else in life, it will challenge you and force you to stretch your comfort zone. Remember, failure is not an option, so don't give up. The only time you really fail is when you quit.

Defining Behavior Styles

To understand behavior styles, begin by realizing that the way a person acts is founded in his or her personal values and circumstances at any given moment. As soon as a customer walks through your door, you will start working on determining the behavior style of this person so you can adjust the way you communicate to better match the prospect's needs.

Almost all behavior types in some way lead back to the DISC profiling system. As in the rest of my training, I attempt to keep things simple. So, I break the behavior types into the following four categories:

- Driver: Action oriented
- Talker: Motivator
- Thinker: Detail oriented
- Relater: Supportive

Let's take a closer look at these four behavior types and how understanding them can help the sales process. As a side note, becoming familiar with the different behavior types will also benefit you in other aspects of your business and personal life.

The Driver

The Driver is the action-oriented decision maker. Those who share the Driver's style tend to be goal driven. They speak in short sentences, often filled with action words. They like to get to the point, and then they move on. They rarely engage in idle conversation. Drivers thrive on the thrill of the challenge, and they have the internal motivation to succeed. Drivers are practical folks who focus on getting results.

The Driver will lead from the front. Picture the general on the battlefield leading the charge. Be prepared to move quickly, as the Driver only knows two speeds – fast and faster. He will question and challenge you. Do not be surprised if the Driver interrupts you in the middle of a sentence. The Driver will disagree with you and even raise his voice at times. You have to remember that you cannot take this personally. A good way to explain the Driver is that he does not want a forty-hour work week, but rather a forty-hour work day!

The Talker

The next behavior type to consider is the Talker, who wants above all else to influence people. The Talker is outgoing and enthusiastic, with a high energy level. Talkers are great idea generators, but often do not have the ability to see an idea through to completion. They enjoy helping others and are particularly fond of socializing. They are usually slow to reach a decision. The Talker is easy to approach, but other styles might criticize him for socializing too much. Talkers are the life of the party. They are your social butterflies. As much as they want to hear your story, they want to tell their own even more. They want to be your friend. If you are extremely busy, you do not want to cross paths with the Talker at the water fountain or the break room. Be friendly with the Talker, and you will create an instantaneous friendship.

The Relater

Relaters are dependable, loyal, and easygoing. They like things to be non-threatening and friendly. They hate dealing with impersonal details and cold hard facts. They are usually slow to reach a decision, and prefer not to be the primary decision maker. They are great team players. Relaters are very often the best listeners and do very well in the P-Effect sales process. Relaters are often described as warm and sensitive to the feelings of others.

The Relater is very patient. In times of great stress or crisis, the Relater will back away from the crisis, but remain patient. Relaters shy away from aggressive behavior and communication styles.

The Thinker

The final behavior style is the Thinker, whose outstanding characteristic is conscientiousness. Thinkers are known for being systematic, well-organized, and deliberate. These individuals appreciate facts and information presented in a logical manner, and require documentation of truth. They enjoy organization and are detail-oriented. They may seem too cautious and overly structured at times. They expect things to be done by the book. Thinkers appreciate agendas and expect you to stick to them. If you present them with facts, you'd better be ready to back them up with proof.

When the program you're involved with requires analysis, the Thinker is the person to ask. Thinkers are fantastic planners, and they weigh and test options carefully before implementing a change. The Thinker has a place for everything and wants everything in its place.

They are certainly not the life of the party, but if a Thinker says he will be there, you can count on his presence . . . and he will be on time. Regardless of the amount of information you give the Thinker, he will very rarely make an on-the-spot decision. If you expect a quick decision from a Thinker, you will be sorely disappointed.

How Styles Interact

Have you tried to determine which behavior style applies to you? If not, think about the list above. Once you have identified your own style, consider how you relate to those with different behavior styles. Here are some ways in which the different styles interact with each other.

Driver/Relater

The Driver is able to work well with the Relater because he appreciates loyalty and dependability. The Relater needs more time than the Driver to make decisions, and that may be a problem in the relationship between people with these two styles, because The Driver can be intimidating and domineering.

Driver/Talker

The Talker often works well with the Driver, because the Talker allows others to make decisions, which the Driver is happy to do. The Talker may be too social for the Driver's taste, however. The Driver likes the support that he feels from the Talker, but the Driver's unsociable disposition may lead to annoyance, which does not work well with the Talker.

Driver/Thinker

The Thinker works well with the Driver when the Thinker is able to provide detailed information that the Driver can use. But the process the Thinker takes to gather facts is too long for the Driver, who may easily become impatient.

Relater/Talker

The Relater is a good listener, and therefore does well with the Talker. The Talker is all about having fun and making friends, whereas the Relater avoids popularity contests. The Talker likes fun and has a motivating spirit.

Talker/Thinker

The Talker overwhelms the Thinker with his high energy. The Thinker is glad to be able to handle detailed tasks, and the Talker is happy to let him.

Thinker/Relater

The Thinker is impersonal and lacks sensitivity, whereas the Relater is all about other people. The lack of daily interaction with others is unacceptable to the Relater. The Relater can be too emotional for the Thinker. However, the Thinker and the Relater are alike in that they are both detail-oriented and slow to make decisions.

Selling Based on Behavior Styles

All of this information is important for you to absorb, but you also need to take the process one step further. You need to ask yourself how to sell to each behavioral type. When you accomplish this, you will be well on your way to understanding how to turn a situation that could result in a lost sale into one with a successful outcome.

Selling to the Driver

The Driver is a person who wants to be in control, to make decisions. If you are dealing with a Driver as your prospect, you will need to ask questions that get this person to open up. It may be challenging. You will find that this person will take more time to build a rapport with. Additionally, you will probably not build the same level of rapport with the Driver as you will with some of the other behavior types.

When working with this person, do not ramble. You do not want to go on and on. Rather, give a short and to-the-point version of whatever information you need to convey. This will be critical.

Perhaps most important is to allow the Driver to be in charge. Allow the Driver to steer conversations so that he can feel in control.

When discussing the senior community with the Driver, ask pointed questions. Ask questions about the prospect's accomplishments. Ask directly what information the Driver needs: "What information can I give you to help you to make a timely decision?" The Driver wants the facts up front and will be making a quick decision.

Here is a summary of some important tips to consider when dealing with Drivers:

Ask questions that will get them talking about themselves.

Spend less time building rapport. This does not mean to skip the rapport-building step. The more rapport you build with the Driver, the better. The Driver does not think he wants to build rapport, but will appreciate it in the end. This is often the discriminating factor between you and your competitor.

Don't ramble. Details should be the *Reader's Digest* version.

Let the Driver feel "in charge." You still need to control the sales process and you will do this by the questions you ask, the skill you use in asking, and the timeliness of the questions. The goal is for the Driver to feel like he is running the show, even though we know better.

Here are some questions you might ask a Driver throughout the sales process:

- How do you manage to get so much done?
- What are some things that have helped you get where you are today?
- What is the best information I can provide so you can make a timely decision?
- What would you like to see accomplished in this meeting?

Now, before moving on, take a few minutes and write down some questions you would feel comfortable asking a Driver. Remember, this is what will make the P-Effect sales process unique to you.

My Questions I Will Ask Drivers

What is the most important thing to you about _____ ?

funding a senior community? _____ ?

What are the concerns you have about a move ?

_____ ?

_____ ?

Selling to the Talker

Selling to Talkers is different. Since these people love to be social, you often find them going on and on. Your part should be the role of the listener, for the most part. It will take you far less time to develop rapport with the Talker. In a recent training session, I asked the group what they thought would be a good question or statement directed at Talkers to get them to open up and start sharing. A response from one of the attendees was, "Hello." We all got a good laugh from that, but how far from the truth is that? Not very far in, most cases.

One of the best ways to sell to Talkers is to relate by sharing your own experiences. Connect with them about the experience of putting a parent into a senior living community. It is always a good idea to use words such as "I feel" in the conversation, but avoid putting thoughts into their minds. Avoid "I think" statements.

You may find that you are becoming friends. This is natural with talkers, and you should not be afraid of getting close. Remember, a Talker can never have too many friends. You will need to plan on spending more time with a Talker, as this is someone who will have something to share about every topic you bring up.

When asking questions to Talkers, you need to know what gets them going. Ask questions about what they enjoy, and about family and children. Get to know their needs. If the senior is sitting in front of you, ask about her grandchildren, other family members, and about the senior herself. You want to be friendly. Ask about her weekend. Get her talking.

Here are some important tips to consider when dealing with Talkers:

- Be an active listener. Take good notes so you can ask questions about what they are sharing.
- Build rapport. This will be easy.
- Relate by sharing your own experiences.
- Use words like "I feel" and less of "I think."
- Don't be afraid to become their friend.

Here are some questions you might ask a Talker throughout the sales process:

- What group activities do you enjoy?
- Tell me more about your children/family.
- What do you like to do for fun?
- What did you do this weekend?

Before moving on, take a few minutes to write down some questions you would feel comfortable asking a Talker. Remember, this is what will make the P-Effect sales process unique to you.

My Questions I Will Ask Talkers

What are you looking for in a Denver community ?

How do you typically spend your day ?

_____ ?

_____ ?

_____ ?

Selling to the Relater

To sell to Relaters, you need to understand their desire to be your friend and to be part of a team. Most Relaters work well with others because they like and trust people. This person does require a bit more time to build rapport with, since they may still question this relationship.

When you have this kind of prospect in front of you at the community, you will need to allow plenty of time. You do not want to rush in with an application or ask them which floor plan is the one they want. You will need to find a way to demonstrate to this person how the solution (moving into the community) will benefit the team (the spouse, the family, friends, etc.).

When talking to Relaters, be sure to use words like "fair" and "your team" and be sure to get to a softer level with them. Lower your voice and be receptive, but still be the leader in the conversation.

Ask the Relater questions about how a decision to move into the community will affect his family. Ask questions, but also be complimentary. Relaters are very organized, so you can ask questions regarding their great organizations skills.

Here are some important tips to consider when dealing with Relaters:

- Realize that they want to like and trust you.
- Spend more time building rapport.
- Take your time and don't rush the sales process.
- Demonstrate how the solution will benefit "the team."

Here are some questions you might ask a Relater during the sales process:

- How will this decision affect your family?
- How do you keep everything looking so nice?
- How are you able to juggle so many responsibilities?
- How do you balance your work/family?

Now, before moving on, take a few minutes and write down some questions you would feel comfortable asking a Relater. Remember, this is what will make the P-Effect sales process unique to you.

My Questions I Will Ask Relaters

_____?

_____?

_____?

_____?

_____?

Selling to the Thinker

When it is a Thinker you are dealing with, you need to take your time going through the process of explaining the community, the benefits, and the overall details of the experience. With these people, you will spend more time explaining facts and details than you will with most other aspects of the sales process.

When talking to the Thinker, be more intellectually oriented and avoid emotional issues in the conversation. Thinkers are not interested in emotions – at least they don't think they are. You will want to use words like "I think" when you are working with a Thinker, rather than using "I feel" sentences.

You need to build credibility with Thinkers. They are looking at you wondering why they should work with you. Remember, with Thinkers, they are not going to make a decision overnight. They want to gather all the facts and compare you against every community in the Western Hemisphere.

Here are some important tips to consider when dealing with Thinkers:

- Take your time going through the process.
- Spend more time with facts and details (have supporting documentation).
- Be intellectually oriented – not emotionally oriented.
- Use words like "I think" and less of "I feel."
- Build credibility.

Here are some questions you might ask a Thinker throughout the sales process:

- What information do you need to make your decision?
- Have I provided you with sufficient information?
- What information can I provide that will be most helpful to you?
- When do you plan to make a decision?

Now, before moving on, take a few minutes to write down some questions you would feel comfortable asking a Thinker. Remember, this is what will make the P-Effect sales process unique to you.

My Questions I Will Ask the Thinker

_____?

_____?

_____?

_____?

_____?

The better you understand each of these behavior types and how to sell to them, the better your sales presentation is going to be. Identify your own behavior traits and those of your prospect so you can better plan for moving the sales process forward. You cannot know how to deal with others until you understand what to expect from yourself.

Learning to identify the Thinker, Driver, Relater, and Talker may require some practice. Use role-play exercises. This is a great way for you and your coworkers to work together as a team. Learn to sell to any behavior type that walks through your door. If and when you put all this together, you will be well on your way to selling more effectively. You are listening to the person's needs and making sure your presentation specifically addresses those needs.

It won't be easy training the mind to automatically recognize these behavior types. The idea is to train when you are not in front of a prospect. Practice by identifying the styles among your family members, coworkers, and friends. At your next social event, sit back and consciously observe people, taking into account their dress, their actions, how and with whom they converse, and so on. You'll be amazed at how quickly people reveal their predominant style. The more you do this, the better your subconscious mind will begin to respond when confronted with the different types. You might actually have fun! Here are some real world scenarios to give you a better understanding of the different behavior types:

Reading a Newspaper

- Talkers look for stories about the party they attended the previous night. They do things that get themselves in the paper. They scan the entire paper looking for interesting current-event articles. They read the entertainment section.
- Drivers mainly read the headlines and the business section. They then turn to the sports section to read about athletic accomplishments.
- Thinkers will call the newspaper if a word is incorrectly spelled or a story is inaccurate.
- Relaters look for a popular current event story to discuss at the office water cooler. They check the obituaries to see if anyone they know has died.

Golfing

- Talkers spend more time in the clubhouse socializing and welcoming new members. Their "almost a hole in one" story is repeated frequently for the benefit of new members.
- Drivers drive the cart and frequently try to move ahead of the golfers in front of them.
- Thinkers keep score for the group and often refer to the rule book. They keep their clubs clean, too.
- Relaters play regularly with the same foursome, usually offering to buy the beverages at the nineteenth hole.

Grocery Shopping

- Talkers approach the "fewer than nine items" checkout line, begin a conversation, and compare the fun stuff in other shopping carts. They hold up the line by conversing with the cashier about upcoming holidays.
- Drivers barrel through the "fewer than nine items" line with fifteen items. After all, it was the shortest line.
- Thinkers approach the same checkout line wrestling with the correct thing to do. "Are the eggs one item, or twelve?" They also count items in other carts, and if they are over the limit, they become irritated.
- Relaters approach the "fewer than nine items" line, count the items, and take comfort knowing they have only eight. If they have ten items, they move to another line.

The Desk

- Talkers say, "I'm busy right now. Give me a few minutes and I'll get back to you." They don't know where the item is on their desk, but won't admit it.
- Drivers have a clean desk, one file out at a time. Nothing else is on the desk. Even their telephone is on the credenza behind them.
- Thinkers say, "It's the third report down in that pile." The desk is messy with Post-it notes and files everywhere, but they know exactly where everything is.
- Relaters have everything in place, with the most impressive, business-related file in full view. A family picture and a picture of the Relater shaking hands with a celebrity is in a prominent position. Relaters have a separate table for visitors, rather than having them sitting at their desk.

Cooking

- Talkers like to cook for groups. They prepare an extra place at the table, just in case company stops by. They go out rather than cook for one.
- Drivers can't cook without a microwave. They buy single portions. Cooking is viewed as a functional necessity, not a social event.
- Thinkers cook with a cookbook, a timer, and a measuring cup. They follow instructions exactly, with no deviations allowed.
- Relaters like to prepare a meal from scratch using a dozen standard recipes, taking the best from each and using the most popular ingredients.

Elevators

- Talkers let everyone in, saying, "Always room for one more, the more the merrier." They ignore the "max limit" sign and hand out business cards on the way down.
- Drivers walk up, push the button, wait impatiently, get in, and speak to no one. If running late, they take the stairs.
- Thinkers enter the elevator, and if it's crowded, they count the number of people. If over the limit, they will ask someone to leave.
- Relaters hold the door for others and ensure they're the last ones on, in case it's full. They don't want to crowd anybody. If necessary to avoid crowding, they will wait for the next elevator. They smile at everyone on the trip down.

Have fun while you are learning. Be prepared to engage in a conversation, regardless of the prospect's behavior type.

This brings up another important aspect of the process: listening.

Improving Your Ability to Listen

You spend countless hours of your day interacting with other people. You know exactly what you want to say and what you want the prospective resident to say. But, do you take the time to listen? Do you know what the person in the elevator said to you today? Do you remember what the resident you passed in the hallway told you about her grandchild? Are you just hearing, or are you listening? Your prospective client can tell the difference.

While many seminars talk about asking the right questions, many fail to provide enough information on how to actually listen to the answers. Questions are a valuable part of the process. However, you have to know what to do after you ask the questions. Listening will tell you.

The following are some tips to help you learn how to listen better. Incorporate these into the sales presentation, following the P-Effect method, and you will see results.

Listen to stories first. Many times, prospective clients come in with concerns and issues. This is a huge decision in their life. They want to tell you their story to get validation of why they are there. **Listen to them.** The stories they tell will contain key information you will want to address during the sales process.

Avoid interrupting your prospective residents. Allow them to finish what they have to say. You cannot listen and talk at the same time. You also do not want to interject your own views and comments into what they are saying. Give them time to tell you all they need to. Then, offer your information or thoughts when they pause in what they are saying.

Listen for the psychological needs of your prospective resident. Most of the time, those who are considering your community need more than just a place to live. They often will drop information or clues to you about what those needs are when they talk. Why are they there? For example, prospective residents may be looking for reassurance that they are doing the right thing by considering senior housing. Maybe they just need more socialization. Perhaps they need assistance with the activities of daily living (ADL).

Listen for the main ideas in what each person is telling you. This will require you to ask questions. Drill down and discover the emotions behind the needs.

As you sit there and listen to an elderly person tell you his or her life story, it is quite natural to become distracted. That phone in the distance is catching your attention. You may be thinking about what you are going to do for dinner. Maybe you are planning your weekend. It is easy to lose focus on what the person is saying. The only way to overcome this is to train yourself to listen intently to the person's words. Create a situation in which there are fewer distractions by turning the computer off and closing the door.

Avoid reacting to the person. Instead, react to the message. You do not want to allow your mental impression of the person to influence the way you interpret the message. As you are listening, do have a pen and paper handy and take notes. Ask for permission to take notes. Don't try to capture every word the prospect is saying. Only write words or phrases down, not every detail. You need to be listening, though. Circle the key words or phrases you want to ask questions about. It is important to find out what the person is interested in and ask probing questions.

When listening, be selective in what you hear. In other words, you want to uncover the critical message of the prospect. What does he need? What is she telling me that can help me to satisfy her needs right now? Be relaxed and open. This allows the prospect to feel more relaxed when talking to you, too. If you do this, the prospect is likely to tell you more.

You never want to be critical of the other person, either mentally or verbally. You need to see the situation from the viewpoint of the other person. Regardless of the circumstances and concerns of the other person, realize that he or she is dealing with a life-changing situation right now. Show compassion.

Here are some tips to help you listen intently for the message the prospect is communicating.

- Face customers when you talk to them.
- Keep your legs and your arms uncrossed. This conveys that you are open to what they are saying.
- Lean slightly forward toward the customer.
- If you are talking to the prospect on the phone, be sure that the meeting area is quiet and private, and that it allows you to close the doors to prevent distractions.
- Ask questions that allow the other person to give feelings, thoughts, and opinions.
- Use open-ended questions when speaking. Everything they tell you is going to be valuable to you in the managed presentation portion of your sales presentation.
- Ask "How can I help you?" and questions such as "Where do we go from here?"
- When they answer a question, ask questions about their answers.
- Be genuinely interested in the person. Don't try to fake it. The prospect may be old, but old is not dumb.

Improving your ability to listen to other people will help you improve the way you present your community to them. If you do not customize your sales presentation to the information and feelings that your customers are providing to you, you will lose them. If you are distracted, rude, or too focused on spitting out features rather than benefits, you will find yourself failing to turn meetings into sales.

Listen and you just might hear exactly what you need to hear in order to achieve success – turning a prospective client into a resident at your community.

In summary:

- Realize that you need to see sales as a business you are running, not as a job you are doing for a weekly paycheck.
- Realize that people are different in many ways, including the way they interact with each other. Behavior styles are critical to understand.
- Once you know what your behavior style is, you can better see what the behavior styles of others are.
- Take the time to learn how to apply the information you have learned about a person through attentive listening.

Use the tips and strategies presented thus far to help you customize your sales presentation. Determine the types of questions you need to ask based on the behavior style of the person you are talking to. Listen and communicate fully in order to achieve your goal of turning a prospective resident into a resident who not only will feel right at home at your community but will be happy to tell others about you as well.

Chapter 10

I'm Just Looking

> *The harder you work, the harder it is to surrender.*
> ~Vince Lombardi

Rarely do people walk into the community just because they are "just looking" or have nothing else better to do. People do not normally wake up and decide to go look at senior living communities just for fun. The key word is rarely, because there are times when some people come just out of curiosity.

Allow me to introduce Harry. I was coaching a couple of salespeople at a community in Georgia when the concierge interrupted us to say that someone was there wanting information. Stephanie said she would help him. I walked out with her and was introduced as the new guy in training. We sat down with Harry in a private area, and Stephanie began to ask him questions. Since I was "the new guy in training," my role was just to observe. After the prospect left, we would discuss the situation.

Harry had dropped his wife off to visit her sister on the Assisted Living side of the community, so he figured he would stop in and kill some time and find out what Independent Living was all about. He and his wife resided in Pittsburg, Pennsylvania, in a neighborhood where their children and grandchildren also lived. They came to Georgia every year for about four or five months at a time, but had no desire to move there permanently. Harry had retired from the military and had been a government contractor. We learned that he and his wife enjoyed watching British movies for fun.

From the beginning, I recognized Harry as a Thinker. Instead of drilling down and probing more with questions, Stephanie would ask a question and then keep moving right along. Although she was trying to strike up a conversation and get Harry talking, she could not get beyond the surface. So, I did something I do not normally do. I decided to take over to give an example of how the process should work.

To get people talking, you don't have to find something you have in common. All you have to do is to be genuinely interested in the person. To clarify, this does not mean you have to be interested in *what* the person is interested in, but *why*. For example, I have no interest in cars whatsoever. However, if I am talking to someone who loves working on cars, I am interested in finding out why he is so interested in cars. That was the approach I took with Harry.

Although I love movies, I am not a fan of foreign films at all. However, when Harry mentioned the British films, he kind of lit up. So, I began to dig a little deeper. After a couple more questions, I learned that Harry subscribed to Netflix. I had an idea what Netflix was, but after hearing Harry talk about it, it made me want to be a customer. Harry should be the poster child for Netflix. We talked for quite a while about Netflix and British movies.

I made several attempts to change the subject to see if there were any other interests. Since we both had the military in common, I brought that up. Nothing. I had worked at the Pentagon as a contractor, so I brought that up, since we had both been contractors. Nothing. Since his football team had just beaten my team the previous year, I tried to add some humor by bringing that up. Nothing. Harry was not interested. He just wanted to talk about British movies and Netflix. So, we did. We talked for about an hour.

I was very proud of Stephanie that she never offered to take him on a tour. That was not the close. We stepped out into the lobby area and continued our conversation. We were laughing and having a great time. One of the residents walked up to us and said, "I don't know what you're doing or talking about, but I want to join in. It sounds like a lot of fun."

As we were saying our good-byes, Harry said he thought he would like to bring his wife by for a visit. Stephanie asked Harry if she could call him in a couple days to set up an appointment if she had not heard from him. He handed Stephanie his phone and said, "Yes. Please put your name and phone number in my phone so when you call, I'll know it's you and be sure to pick up." Then he left.

We went back and joined the other sales agents and debriefed them on what had happened. Stephanie shared her feelings: "Mike I was really upset when you took over, because I thought you didn't trust me. However, after a minute, I was glad you had. I was asking random questions trying to find something I could relate to. Since I do not like foreign movies, I completely flew over that question. It was magical watching you get Harry to open up with just a few probing questions."

I was flying back home that day. When I arrived at the airport, I went online and found an old British movie that I was hoping Harry had not seen. I sent the information to Stephanie and told her to buy the DVD and have it delivered to Harry at his hotel.

Three days later, I got an email from Stephanie saying Harry and his wife were coming for a tour. About a week later, I received another email from Stephanie. All it said was, "Guess who just put a deposit down on a cottage?"

Here is the point to the story. Treat everyone walking through the door as a hot lead, even those who say they are not planning on making a move. You never know what might happen. How many times have you made a purchase when you were only planning to look? Besides, if nothing else, the "looker" could be your next referral source.

Asking at the Right Time

It's not enough just to ask questions. Asking the correct questions is a science. Asking the correct questions at the correct time is an art. I was on a tour with Amy and the Smiths. Like most salespeople, Amy had not succeeded in establishing rapport with the couple. Although she found out some basic needs of the Smiths, she never really drilled down. We were sitting in the community coffee shop having a discussion prior to the tour. Amy was not doing a particularly poor job, but her tour just sounded like every other tour I shadow. There was nothing special about the visit.

After answering several questions, Mr. Smith asked about security. Amy responded that the community was gated and a security guard was on call if needed. Then Amy proceeded to ask the Smiths if they wanted to go and see a couple of apartments. Since Amy had not narrowed down the exact needs, we visited three different floor plans. Upon entering the first model on the ground floor, Mr. Smith noticed a door that provided access to the back of the house. He asked if there was a similar door in the master bedroom, and Amy said no. The door was part of the original construction plans to allow access to the workers. It was the only model with the access door. Mr. Smith simply responded, "Good."

Now, I don't know about you, but I am seeing a pattern. In the coffee shop, Mr. Smith had a question regarding security. If a prospect brings a subject up, it is obviously a real concern. Amy ignored it at the time. Then Mr. Smith brought it up again in the model. Once again, a quick answer and nothing else. I am chomping at the bit to say something, but I bite my tongue. We finally make it to the third model on the top floor. I can tell that Mr. Smith is interested. Although Mrs. Smith has been on the tour, she has said very little – at least to me. As we were walking to different models, Amy walked ahead with Mrs. Smith and I walked behind with Mr. Smith. That gave Mr. Smith and me the opportunity to chat (what I like to call building rapport). In that short period of time, I learned that Mr. Smith was having some medical difficulties, which was the reason they were looking to make a change in their living situation. I also learned that they had put the house on the market right before they started researching senior living. They were hoping to sell the home prior to moving into a community.

Mr. Smith did not provide much insight into his medical condition, but he did seem concerned about it. I chose not to push it any further. That was the art in the questioning skill. We arrived into the third model, and the Smiths took about five minutes to tour. I sat down in the living room chair that was adjacent to the dining room area. I wanted to stay out of the way and let Amy do her job.

They walked out of the second bedroom, and Mrs. Smith sat down on the couch. In my mind, I was thinking, *Yes, I think we can help these folks.* Mr. Smith chose to stand in the dining room area. He leaned against the kitchen bar and gazed into the kitchen. There was a cabinet blocking my view so I couldn't see into the kitchen to identify what was so intriguing. Then I realized he wasn't looking at anything. He was deep in thought. So, I broke my rule and jumped in. Here is how the conversation went:

Me: "Mr. Smith, how do you want to feel when you move into your new home?"

<Mr. Smith slowly turns his head toward me and just stares at me. After a long pause he continues.>

Mr. Smith: "I really don't know how to answer that question. No one has ever asked me that question before."

<I remain silent. About a minute later with tears in his eyes he begins.>

"I told you I had some medical issues. Without going into detail, they are pretty serious. The main reason I want to move into a community is because I want to make sure my wife is taken care of when I'm gone. I want her to continue to socialize with our friends, and I know we will make some new friends wherever we go who will be a support group for her."

Me: "Mr. Smith, why is it important for your wife to have a support group and continue to socialize?"

Mr. Smith: "Mike, I am scared that when I am gone, she will shut herself away from everyone. We're so used to hanging out with my friends, I know she's going to get lonely, and I don't want her to feel that way."

Me: "Mr. Smith, I can't imagine how you must feel right now. However, I do know that if something were to happen to me, I would want the same things for my wife. I have been both scared and lonely in my life, and I would rather not ever feel that way again, if given the choice. Is it okay if I ask you another question?"

I then asked about security. I learned that they suspected their home had been broken into when they were out of town for the weekend. Although they were not sure, the back door was unlocked, and Mr. Smith was quite sure he had locked it. Once again, he did not want his wife to have to worry about being afraid. It didn't matter whether he forgot to lock the door or not. What mattered is how he felt. His perception was his reality.

I asked Mr. Smith to come over and join his wife on the couch, and I asked Mrs. Smith how she felt about what she had just heard. She broke down and started crying. By that time, Amy was in tears, and I had a couple of tears running down my face, too. Mrs. Smith only spoke for a couple minutes, but the love the couple shared was obvious. Neither of them wanted the other to experience anything but peace and joy.

I wiped a tear from my cheek and said, "Mr. Smith, what is the most important thing we can do today to help you?"

He reached into his pocket, pulled out his checkbook, and asked, "Who do I make the check out to? You helped us come to the understanding that we need to do something before it's too late."

I replied, "Mr. Smith, you said you needed to sell your home first. We would be happy to take the deposit to hold the apartment for you until you sell your home."

He got a mischievous smile across his face and said, "Awwww, I was just joshing. I wanted to have an ace up my sleeve, just in case. How much should I write the check for to cover my first two months?"

This really happened. Do you think I ever asked that leading question again? You'd better believe it. I don't ask it just because the prospect has to really think about the answer. I don't ask it just because it leads us into the emotional level. I ask it because I genuinely care about how they want to feel when they move into their new home.

There was a right time to ask that question. It would not have been nearly as effective in the coffee shop. When he mentioned fear and loneliness, I knew I had gone below the surface and reached his heart. I received an email a couple of months ago, and was saddened to learn of Mr. Smith's death. However, Mrs. Smith had her friends and was coping very well. I know Mr. Smith would be happy!

We had been able to give him the peace of mind he needed in his final weeks.

Amy has not been the same person since that tour. As I was leaving the community that evening, she hugged me and said, "Mike, you changed my life. I really do care about these residents, but I was just not showing it. I seemed more concerned about going through the motions, the way I was taught early in my career. I am committed to making a change."

Amy is now one of the top performing salespeople in her company. Out of over 200 salespeople, she is consistently at the top. She truly has stopped selling and started caring.

Chapter 11

The P-Effect for Your Organization

> *Confidence is contagious and so is lack of confidence, and a customer will recognize both.* ~Vince Lombardi

Up to this point we have provided a great deal of information on what the P-Effect is and have presented tips and strategies to begin the process. However, implementing P-Effect into your organization requires that you have a full understanding of the entire process.

This is the only way that you can improve your overall sales margin. If you want to have your community at near a hundred percent occupancy, you need to be using P-Effect.
In this chapter, we break down the system and teach the steps to apply the P-Effect to the senior housing industry, specifically to assisted living, senior communities, and similar types of housing.

Building Rapport

As we discussed earlier, the first concept of the P-Effect is to build rapport. Rapport is the foundation of every relationship, and it is critical in the development of a sense of trust between you and the prospect. Rapport starts at the "hello" and it needs to carry on throughout the entire call.

Show genuine interest in your prospect. It does not matter what you know until you can demonstrate how much you care. Remember, most people walking in your door are making a major life decision. They do not want to do this with someone they do not trust.

Ask probing and natural questions. Questions provide you not only with helpful information but also an opportunity to connect with the prospect. "My father has fallen three times in the last month. We are concerned." You might reply, "I'm so sorry to hear about that. Have his doctors uncovered what is causing the falls?"

Listen and listen more. This is not the time to talk, but to listen. Ask the right questions, and your prospect will open up and tell you what he or she feels, knows, and needs help with. Focus solely on the customer during this interaction. There is nothing more important than the words coming out of the prospective resident's mouth! Remember that during this initial contact, you are also gathering information to help you to determine the prospects' behavioral style. Then, you know how to respond and work with them.

Rapport is something that may at times seem to happen instantaneously, but more often, it develops over a short amount of time. Whereas trust takes a longer time to build, establishing rapport is simply finding some common ground with a person. In order for someone to trust you, he or she will need enough experience with you to learn about your integrity, professionalism, honesty, and consistency.

Building Credibility

The next element of the P-Effect to focus on is building credibility. It would be great if everyone could trust everyone else, and there was no need to feel that "something" that makes you say, "Wait a minute . . . is this for real?" People usually do not trust other people right out of the door. They need time to build up to that point.

Credibility can lead to trust, and trust is critical to persuasion. Credibility implies a commitment to truth, fairness, and objectivity. In the community environment, there are several things to understand about credibility. First, you will seem more credible if you focus on the benefits of the product you have to offer. Instead of harping about what the other guys do not have, focus solely on providing information about the community you represent. This shows you are credible, not playing the *I'm better than the next guy* game.

Know which features of your community will benefit the prospect you are working with. For example, if an adult child mentions concerns about the diet of the parent not being nutritious, you can emphasize the community dining center. The direct result of this will be a building of credibility.

Know what sets your company apart from the rest. What is your different and better story? Explore the advantages of your business. Know them so you can show that your community is better than others, but do so in a positive manner, without criticizing the competition.

Credibility is essential, and once it is broken, it takes a long time and a lot of work to rebuild. Building credibility requires working with people as individuals. In other words,

applying behavioral flexibility, based on the style information you have learned.

Along with this, remember the value of stretching your
comfort zone. No, it is not easy to do, and it definitely will
provide you with some frustration along the way. But the
goal on the other side is well worth the work. If you plan to
implement behavioral flexibility, you need to be willing to
stretch that comfort zone.

Who is the best salesperson? Is it the person who makes the
most money? Is it the guy with the years of experience
under his belt? No, it is the person who is able to change and
adapt to people – specifically, to each of the prospects that
come into your office, sit at your desk, and wait for you to
tell them why your community is going to be their next
home. No matter what your own style of behavior, your
ability to alter your behavior style to match the other's needs
is what will make you successful.

Discovering Urgency

The next step in moving toward P-Effect is to discover
urgency. First, let us define what urgency really is: Something that is urgent requires immediate action or attention. It
is compelling. It conveys a sense of pressing importance. It
is a force or impulse that impels or constrains.

Often something tragic, dangerous, or disturbing has happened: A parent has fallen. A spouse has died. One of the
questions on the inquiry sheet provided earlier asks the
prospect, *What made you come into this community today?*
Or, *What made you call today?*

Most of the time, there is a reason this person came in at this time, today, not yesterday, not tomorrow. Something compelled him to act now. It is part of your job to find out what that urgency is. In fact, by getting the prospect to answer the question regarding urgency, you can usually count on that person closing with you if you demonstrate your community's ability to overcome the problem that created the urgency. Here is a great tool to help you determine urgency with a prospect. It's a three step process, and when you master it, your close will become much easier.

- Determine the prospect's situation.
- Determine how long the prospect has been in the current situation.
- Find out what has recently happened to compel the prospect to start looking now.

Here are some questions to ask to help you better understand the level of urgency a prospect has right now, even one who may not seem forthcoming.

- When do you need to have your loved one move in?
- When are you planning to make the move?
- When do you plan to move in and start taking advantage of the benefits we offer?
- What made you pick up the phone and call me today?
- Where are you at in the decision-making process right now?
- Are you in a hurry? Do you need to find some place right away? (This is especially helpful when a loved one is in a hospital setting.)
- What is your timetable? When do you want us to be ready for you?
- How much longer can you put off this decision?

Each of these questions can help you to learn the reason behind the call. It is in getting an answer to these questions that you will find your prospect willing to say, "Here is what I need and why I need it. Can you help me?"

Identifying Needs

We have discussed this topic throughout this book. Why is there so much emphasis on it? This is your trigger, your tool to make a person say, "Hey, this guy has exactly what I need and there is no reason to look farther." You have taken the time to establish a rapport with the person. The prospect trusts you now, at least to some degree. You have built the beginnings of a relationship. You respect the person, and the person respects you. Now, you need to find out what the hot buttons are. Here is why:

Value = Hot Button = Decision

Hot buttons are the values or emotions that drive the behaviors and decisions of your prospect. Learn what these are if you plan to increase your sales and become a true sales warrior. This is the foundation of success that will help you to achieve your one hundred percent occupancy goal.

Here is what you need to know about hot buttons:

- You need to find out what about your community center is important to the prospect who has called you or stopped in.
- You need to determine which of the features and benefits your community center offers that are going to be important to your prospect.
- You need to find out *why* it is important to the prospect.

After identifying the prospect's hot buttons, you can then help the prospect to make the best decision, an educated decision about whether your community center is right for him or not.

In the selling process, identifying needs is an important step because it will allow you to learn the true motivators behind the prospect's interest. Here are some helpful questions that can help you to get started in this process. There are many ways to phrase a question to elicit the information you need. Remember, we have given you some additional options in the sales inquiry sheet we provided earlier in this book.

- What amenities are most important to you in a community center?
- What features are you looking for in our policies or plans?
- What would the ideal community for you be like, in a perfect world?
- What is on your wish list? I know you have given this investment a lot of thought, and I want to know what is on the wish list, not just on the must-have list.
- If pricing were not an object, what would be the ideal community center setup for you? What additional services or products could we offer to you?
- What services do you expect at a community center? What features do you expect?
- Describe the perfect community center for your needs.

In most situations, these questions are going to force the person in front of you sitting at your desk, or the person on the phone with you, to open up. Remember, after you get the person in for the tour, you still need to sit down and ask questions. These questions can be helpful to get the potential customer to open up to you again.

Remember, at this point, there is no sales information coming from you. You are not interjecting or offering any type of sales pitch yet. That comes next, and only after you know what is important to the prospect!

Powerful Managed Presentation

Here's something you may not know. When you have done everything in the P-Effect to this point, your sales presentation (your managed presentation) is going to be easy. Many people spend a lot of time worrying about this particular step in the process, but if you have done everything else right up to this point, guess what: this step is already set up to be a success.

Let's recap here. At this point, you have built a relationship with the prospect. You have gained the prospect's trust. You have also identified the hot buttons, or the needs of the prospect. The next step is to show your stuff!

To this point, you have allowed the customer to do most of the talking. You have controlled the process, though, by using your superior questioning skills to guide the conversation and to gather information. Now, it is time to present the various options that your community offers to the prospect. When you work through the managed presentation, you need to present your community's products and services around the specific needs and the desires (the values) that are important to the prospect.

Chapter 12

Confirming the Sale

> *Business is not just doing deals; business is having great products, doing great engineering, and providing tremendous service to customers. Finally, business is a cobweb of human relationships.* ~Ross Perot

Most of the time people buy from people. People love to buy things, but they buy from people based on what those people say or do, or how they act toward the prospect. Think about all the things that buying does for us:

- It satisfies the needs of the ego.
- It helps to elevate our status.
- It satisfies our greed.
- It creates the joy of spending money.
- It fosters peace of mind.

How many more things can you add to that list?

Your job as a sales professional is to turn sales, right? To make this happen, use the P-Effect, which allows you to take a mutual journey of trust, honesty, and respect. You've worked through the P-Effect model to this point, now you just need to confirm the sale.

This is the point where some sales agents will say that you are "closing the sale." Sure, that may be correct at some level, but the term closing does not really belong. It has negative connotations and it brings up thoughts of a creepy sales person waiting in the wings to steal the money out of an innocent child's pocket.

Remember this: traditional closing techniques violate the sales relationship. Your prospect is tired, irritated, and unwilling to deal with your unethical methods of making him sign on the dotted line. He balks, and will not sign.

Instead of doing this kind of close, your job is to *confirm* the sale, using a non-manipulative, straightforward approach, by presenting a practical, valued-added solution. When you confirm a sale, the prospect is handing you a gold medal because you have created a win-win situation for both of you. The problem is that many sales professionals want to jump around to get to this point. Unless you have worked through the P-Effect model, you will not find the closing easy, and you will struggle to confirm the sale.

Overcome Objections and Close

Many of those who want to learn to become sales warriors are waiting for this information. Most believe that this is the hardest part of the sales transaction, and they want tricks, tips, and strategies to help them to overcome this situation. It could happen, but it is just as important to realize that the close is part of the process, not a destination.

What happens when there is an objection? If you have done your job and followed the steps of the P-Effect model, handling objections is not a problem and is easy to do. At this point, the prospect is actually yearning to close. It is now time to ask for the prospect's agreement to move forward, to take the next step in the process.

Objections happen. They *should* happen! Here are some sample closing questions to get the objections to the surface so you can move beyond them.

- Can you think of any reason not to take the next step and become part of our community center?
- Is there anything you can think of that we left out or did not discuss that would keep you from moving forward and becoming part of our community?
- Are there any questions you have or any information I need to clarify for you before you move forward to become a part of our community?

You will notice that these are open-ended questions. They present the opportunity for the prospect to come forward and offer objections. Once you ask the question, there are several things that can happen.

- The prospect has an objection. Repeat the objection.
- The prospect has a question. Ask for clarification of the question.
- Come to an agreement on what the next step will be.

The next step may be:

- To leave a deposit
- To complete an application

- To schedule a follow up appointment
- To schedule a follow up contact

Are Objections That Bad?

When you are considering the objection, you might curl your lip in a snarl and dig deeper into your seat. Objections seem bad, but are they really that bad? Objections do have a bad habit of occurring at places in the sales process that you would not expect them. They can appear out of nowhere, often without any warning.

Look at objections this way: overcoming objections is your ticket to sales success. You will not be able to close the sale until you have resolved the prospect's objections. Most of the time an objection is a smokescreen that the prospect raises against possible buyer's remorse. In the community center, there may be a sense of guilt at being unable to provide for a loved one in another way.

Many sales professionals view sales as a process to trick or otherwise convince a customer to act, so that they can be rid of that customer. When an objection arises, the sales professional feels challenged, because the objection requires on-the-spot thinking to arrive at an unrehearsed response. The canned pitch does not cover the objection, and it is impossible to predict and prepare for every possible objection. Rather than dreading objections, you should view them as an opportunity, and if you have done your P-Effect model properly, you will find no problem in overcoming the objection.

Anticipate and welcome objections. You should be planning for objections just as you do any other portion of the P-Effect model. These are not just an obstacle, but are an asset in the sales process that puts you one step closer to confirming the sale. When you have this positive attitude, you are more likely to respond without any hint of hostility toward the prospect.

To communicate your positive attitude toward the prospect's concerns, use a cushioning statement, or empathy. You may say something such as, "You're right, our price is higher than most, but what exactly is your concern?" When you say something like this, you help to build rapport with the prospect and you encourage the trust-building that is critical for the development of a relationship.

Your reaction to the objection is more important than the objection itself.

How do you respond to objections? What is your attitude toward them? Be honest with yourself. What do you do when you hear an objection?

Do you think to yourself, *What exactly does the prospect mean by that statement?* If so, you are on the right track. It may not be entirely clear what the true objection is. When this happens, ask questions such as:

- Is this what you mean? (Paraphrase what the prospect is saying to you.)
- What do you mean by that?
- Tell me more about that. Please elaborate.
- I'm not sure I understand.

The rule to remember is to never offer a response to an objection until you fully understand how it relates to this particular prospect and this particular situation.

The Cause of the Objection

As you take into consideration the underlying cause of the objection, realize most objections come about for the same reasons. The prospect is unsatisfied, has unanswered questions, or has undeveloped expectations. When you remove the cause of an objection, you remove the concern.

Objections stem from:

- Political reasons (My sister works for your competitor.)
- Personal biases (I prefer to deal with your competitor.)
- Prejudices (I have heard bad things about your company.)

Most objections, however, come from unsatisfied expectations. A person does not want to buy something – especially something that involves such a drastic change as moving into a community development – if he feels uneasy about the person he is working with, the process, or even the community itself. The prospective resident expects to have all concerns handled before agreeing to make such a life-altering change.

Objections mean that the prospect has listened to you and participated in the sales presentation. The objection may just be a means of clarifying a point of concern. Once you, the salesperson, satisfactorily resolves the objection, you can advance the sale.

Here are a few more things you need to know about objections:

- Objections are a means to direct the conversation in line with the customer's needs. Use objections to help you to know what to talk about with your prospects.
- The absence of objections should be cause for concern, since this means the prospect is not listening, bored, or simply not interested.
- When you encounter objections, the prospect will be satisfied with your answer, ask another question, or generate a new objection.

There is a difference between objections and tough questions. A tough question is asked in order to draw information from you, whereas the objection is a comment made about a specific thing you had to say.

The Five Magic Words

The Five Magic Words are the words you need to know to close the sale. How do you confirm the sale? With the P-Effect model, you have a process that is simple to use to get to the confirmation. Many people are surprised that this model works, because it is so simple. But that is what makes it so effective. As you look at the P-Effect model, there are five words you need to know. These are the most powerful words you will ever say to your prospect. Look your customer square in the eye. With confidence with your voice and your body language ask, "May I have your business?"

Then, wait. Do not say anything else until the prospect has responded. That is all there is to it, and if you follow the P-Effect model and use these five words, you are going to see a major improvement in your sales percentage. You can expect to double your closing percentage or better, and you will see occupancy within your community rise to near capacity.

These words work because they are clear, sincere, artless, and professional. Say the words out loud to yourself. Say them again to the mirror. These five words work for all of the four behavioral styles. All four of these styles will appreciate the intention of your question and will react favorably to it.

Is it that easy? Many sales seminars teach gimmicks. You do not have to trick your prospect into working with you. You do not have to memorize weird power closes that do not work properly. All you need to do is to keep the process simple.

It is important to stress that the close is not a one-sided speech. The sales process is not a lecture or a listing of features from a script. It is a two-way conversation in which you learn about the prospect and the prospect learns about what you have to offer and how it meets his or her needs. That is it. Because this relationship is built on trust, you will find that the process works, and it works very well.

The Most Common Reason the Sales Close Fails

Here is a shocking number for you: seventy percent of sales calls end without a direct request by the salesperson for the prospect's business. Confirming is the final effort of the gold medal performance. Remember, second place is the first loser. Some sales people attempt to make the confirmation, but they lack the ability, confidence, or know-how to make it happen. They end up with a weak, unconvincing request to do business.

Here is what a common close sounds like. This is NOT recommended:

Salesperson:　"Is there anything else I can show you or answer for you today?"

Prospect:　"No, thanks. I think you have answered all of my questions. I have the information I need."

Salesperson:　"Okay, then. Let me leave you with our most recent brochure. Will you be available next week?"

Prospect:　"Yes, I will be around."

Salesperson:　"Okay, great. Why don't I give you a call early next week and we can discuss our community again, and see how you feel about it. Is that okay?"

Prospect:　"Sure, that's fine."

That's it. The conversation ends. This is not a strong sales opportunity but mystery shops often show that this is the real, underlying problem. There is no call for action, no direct "I want to do business with you." In this close, the salesperson has avoided the most important question and is leaving with nothing more than hope for another opportunity. But the competition is right there, around the corner, ready to answer and to ask that powerful, five-word question. The competition is waiting and the prospect is still in need. His problem has not been solved. In fact, if he needs to find a solution right away, chances are good that he is not going to wait for your call next week, but will instead check out the competition to see if something is available. You become the backup plan, since he knows he can talk to you in a few days.

By asking for the person's business, you reaffirm the agreement between yourself and the prospect and create an opportunity for both of you to achieve the results you need. The prospect gets into the community center, solving his or her problem. You increase your occupancy rate, boost your self-confidence, and enter the world of the superior sales warrior.

A Journey

Confirming the sale may seem like it is the end point of the buying process, but in fact, it is something you are building on throughout the process. It takes a variety of confirmations during the initial inquiry, the tour, and your presentation to get the buyer sitting with you at this final point. When you get to this point, as a sales warrior, you will be able to easily step into the process of confirming the sale. You can confidently ask for the prospect's business without fearing objections – the "no" answer.

Why is it that so many sales professionals become paralyzed with the thought of closing? Even those who have worked through all of the P-Effect steps may still find themselves worried, even afraid, of what lies ahead. Why does this happen?

We are terrified of rejection, afraid of failing, or worried that we will sound silly to the prospect. We fear upsetting the customer, or fear that we are not good enough to ask the customer for the sale.

Dwelling on any of these thoughts or even allowing them to enter your mind, will compromise the sales process. Fear is learned as a result of negative conditioning experienced throughout life, beginning as early as childhood, from parents to teachers and even siblings. Anyone who has been turned down or has been hurt in the past has had a sense of fear instilled in his mind. Remember those boxes of experiences tucked away in the warehouse of your brain. Some place in there are the triggers that cause you to be afraid when you enter the final phase of confirming the sale.

Many people reject the sales proposal they just offered to the prospect. They doubt the approach, even before they hand over that proposal to the client. There is a direct relationship between low self-esteem with negative self-talk and the lack of confidence to ask for business. Confirming the sale demands an attitude of confidence. You expect the prospect will say yes to you. Anything less than a positive attitude is unhelpful. Assume the sale, and you will get it.

No Does Not Always Mean No

Another problem that many sales professionals have is not knowing the difference between the words "know" and "no." There is a difference, of course, when it comes to English usage, but in the sales profession, there is another big difference between these two words.

When the prospect says no, what do you think he or she is saying?

Does *no* mean total rejection? They think your community is horrible and storm out the door. That is an example of *no*.

Need to know means more information is required. If the prospect says this, he or she is in a situation where you must elaborate on the subject and provide the information necessary to enable the prospect to make a positive buying decision. *Know* does not mean *no*.

When a prospect is sitting at your desk after touring your community and listening to your presentation, does he or she really mean no? In most cases, the word means that the customer has not seen the value of the community center yet and needs to know more about the services you can provide. In this situation, you need to step back and begin to discuss the features that connect with these needs. You may be able to do this by asking the question, *What is the single barrier preventing us from moving forward?* This hands the floor to the prospect, who is now forced to provide you with a reason why he or she is unable to confirm the sale. The potential objections the prospect may offer can help you to see where you did not provide enough needs-focused information about the services your community offers. Until the customer sees value, you will continue to hear the *I need to knows*. These continue to be opportunities for you.

Confirming the Sale: Timing Is Everything

When is the right time to pop the question? This is a frequently asked question, one to which you may be surprised to hear the answer. The answer to this question is "when you have earned the right to ask for the close."

The only time you have the right to confirm the sale is when you have earned the right to do so. It is a privilege. You must earn it. This answer is not as clear-cut and straight-forward as most people want to hear. It remains subject to broad interpretation and is founded on your interpretation of perceived buying signals. However, even if you have not earned the right to ask for the close, ask anyway. Okay, I am going to repeat myself because most salespeople do not earn the right to ask for the close. Even if you have not earned the right to ask for the close, ask anyway! Are you getting it? Ask for the close!

If you read other sales educational material, you may be told to confirm the sale when "the prospect is ready and communicates a buying signal." Another example might be, "When the buyer appears ready."

This is not specific, and it really does not provide the sales warrior with enough information to make the move with confidence. While body language is a part of the process, it is not the sole means of interpreting when to close the sale. Every person is different and just as behavior flexibility suggests, you need to ensure that you close the sale when your prospect is ready for it.

Remember, behavioral styles play a role in nonverbal communication. For example, the Talker will communicate through his or her body language differently than a Driver will, even though both people are thinking the same thing. There is no possibility of creating a universal set of standards to evaluate when a person is ready, based solely on body language. Is body language important? It is not necessarily something that you need to focus on, unless the person's body language changes drastically during the presentation. The only time you need to really take action is when a prospect gets up from your desk and walks away from the meeting.

You are sitting there now thinking, *So when do you know how to confirm the sale, then?* The best time to confirm the sale is after you have moved through the P-Effect model.

- You have developed rapport with the prospect.
- You have developed a level of trust with the prospect.

- The prospect has provided you with honest answers to the open-ended questions you have asked.
- You have presented a presentation that is based on the prospect's specific needs and desires.
- Your presentation meets and exceeds the prospect's needs and desires.

If you have worked through these steps, you have earned the right to ask the question you want and need to ask. Once you ask and the prospect indicates readiness to take the next step, that's great. If the prospect says "know" then it is time to take a few steps back and to work through evaluating needs to match the needs of the prospect to the features and benefits of your community. Every prospect is different. In many cases, prospects just need to know more before they are able to say yes to working with you.

The following are tips that can help you to be ready to confirm the sale:

- During your managed presentation, be sure to bridge at least two appropriate features to benefits with the prospect before you ask the confirming question.
- Show the prospects exactly how what your community has to offer will benefit them or their loved ones.
- Show how the benefits of making the move outweigh the costs. To do this, you need to create value with your prospects throughout the process.
- Remember that a successful confirmation is not an isolated tactic. It is natural outcome of having created value throughout the P-Effect model.
- If you are unable to confirm, for any reason, you did not successfully complete one of the prior steps. You did not build rapport. You did not identify needs, or

you did not present a creative, value-added solution to the prospect's needs.

- Before you do confirm the sale, mentally see the prospect saying yes. Envision the prospect moving in and settling into the community center. See the prospect signing the papers and handing over a deposit.
- After confirming the sale, be quiet. Wait until the prospect responds before you state anything. Allow some time.
- In situations where you cannot persuade a prospect move in, make that person a friend. Interact and be friendly. The worst case scenario is that this person will become a helpful referral source to you in the future.

Are You Proactive?

An important question you need to ask of yourself, "Am I proactive?" Sales counselors need always to be proactive. Here are some examples of being proactive or not. See if any of these apply to you.

Do you show up for sales appointments, including visits with prospects, without knowing what the prospect is looking for? Do you go to meetings like this without any experience in what the prospect actually needs, who the decision makers are, and what their biggest concerns are? If you did not use the sales inquiry sheet provided in this book, chances are good you dropped the ball on this one.

Do you avoid an attempt to close on the next step in the process, but instead request that the prospect actually call when ready to make a decision? Most prospects making such a life-changing decision are scared, and they are not likely to make the change until someone helps them to make it.

During the call or visit, do you forget or just avoid asking for contact information, including phone numbers and email addresses, from prospects? Are you allowing people to sit at home and wait by the phone for your call?

If you have an onsite visit, do you wait seven to ten days to follow up? Within that amount of time, the prospect has likely moved on to another company that was more anxious for his business. When people call to learn about senior housing options, they need answers, and often need to make a decision quickly. The longer you wait, the more time you allow for the competitors to jump in.

Do you get into the prospect's interests deeply enough? Or do you wait too long to do this and lose the prospect's interest?

You should not be reactive, but proactive, acting sooner rather than later, and getting to the heart of the prospect's needs before he or she moves on to the next guy.

Chapter 13

Learn from Doing

> *A life spent making mistakes is not only more honorable*
> *but more useful than a life spent in doing nothing.*
> ~George Bernard Shaw

When you look at the grand scheme of things, you may notice that there are untold amounts of training, consulting, research, books, and articles, all written about how to improve the way people sell. Why does so little of this seem to make a difference or change the way sales managers and companies do business?

We would not write these books or conduct these seminars if people – sales-minded people – were not interested in the topic. The ideas in the books are often accepted, but are rarely implemented. Authors try to twist things around and repackage the same information in a new and updated version, knowing there is always an audience for it.

The goal of each of these authors is the same – to get people to buy the book and implement the strategies it proposes. Many of these books do not teach sales managers anything they do not already know. In fact, most of the time, they contain little that is new. Why do managers keep buying these books, then? It is because knowing or believing is not enough. These sales managers hope that the next book is going to finally change the way they do business and that this will translate into performance in the organization.

The Doing Attitude

We all know people who are full of great ideas, and yet they never act on them, so they accomplish nothing. Then there are those with very bad ideas who are always acting on them, and creating havoc. And finally, there are the people with the right ideas *and* the willingness to act on them, and these are the people who achieve greatness in whatever endeavors they choose. Why the differences, and where do they come from? It's all about attitude. How do we define attitude? It is sometimes hard to pinpoint. I have seen quite a few attempts, but one of the best and most applicable to our subject matter appeared in a recent article by Glenn D. Williams.

Attitudes are unseen, and often unexamined motivations deep within our minds. We all develop these deep motivations so early that we're unaware of the process. Some have suggested that even unborn children are learning attitudes, based on the emotions displayed around them. As we grow, emotional events are recorded in our minds with great importance, forming unconscious motivations for almost every action and reaction later in life. As we live, our experiences either reinforce or alter these motivations. Most of these attitudes are so deeply embedded, we never have to think of them, but they drive how we think and act, almost like remote control.

This is a great working definition that pinpoints the salient aspects of attitude. They are *unseen* and often *unexamined* motivations. They are *unconscious* and *deeply imbedded*. And although we never have to think of them, *they drive how we think and act*. Pretty powerful stuff! How can we use this definition to set ourselves apart from others? Perhaps attitudes, by their nature, must remain unseen, but they certainly don't have to be unexamined. And though many people may be willing to remain unaware of the process by which attitudes are formed, this is another area where we can differentiate ourselves from the crowd. We can train ourselves to become conscious of that process, and use that consciousness to guide the process in the direction we wish it to go. And we can consciously decide whether we want our life experiences to reinforce particular attitudes, or alter them. So although we may never *have* to think of our attitudes, if we want to reach levels of achievement beyond the ordinary, we can choose awareness over unawareness.

Now that we know that we have a certain amount of say as to what kind of attitudes we want to develop, we need to determine how to use that gem of information.

In the business of selling, we need to do more than think about what we must *do*, if we hope to succeed. We can think brilliant thoughts, make endless plans, but where will that get us if another crucial element is lacking: action. Which brings us to the Doing Attitude. What do we mean by a Doing Attitude? Doing is the performing of an action, that very element that we have determined must be present, along with our feelings, thoughts, and knowledge, if we are to succeed.

So ask yourself, do you have a Doing Attitude? Can you take your thoughts, feelings, beliefs, and knowledge and make them work for you and others through your actions? Can you focus your attitude in such a way that your reactions to the people and events in your environment are positive?

Reflect on Beliefs

Our attitudes reflect our underlying beliefs. But if we haven't examined those beliefs and haven't come to terms with them, they may be holding us back. As humans, we can choose to reflect upon our beliefs, and if they are preventing us from going to the place we need to be, we can consciously work toward changing them. And we can consciously choose to delay forming new beliefs by taking a wait-and-see attitude before deciding whether to embrace a particular belief.

Beliefs are simply the thoughts and ideas that one feels to be true, but they may have been formed upon false assumptions. Thoughtful reflection can help you decide which among your beliefs are based on a solid foundation, and which on a flimsy assumption. It can help you decide which beliefs will work for you in life, and which will work against you. And once you have sorted out your beliefs, you can actively work on developing a Doing Attitude.

Ponder this very apt quote from legendary coach Lou Holtz:

Ability is what you're capable of doing. Motivation determines what you do. Attitude determines how well you do it.

Put it to use in your career, and you will achieve more than you ever believed possible.

Satisfaction or Loyalty?

You may be wondering how the "doing" we discuss here relates to your business success. In effect, it really does have everything to do with it. Your experience is what keeps people coming back to you. Your experience keeps the couple in your community talking about you to their friends and family.

Customer loyalty is based on caring, communication, positive expectations, affection, and positive responses. These things cannot happen if you do not "do" them. This is why customer service is so important. If you want your customer service to work, you need to examine what to look for in effective customer service. Effective customer service:

- Accommodates needs.
- Is knowledge-based.
- Reflects a positive attitude.
- Anticipates customer needs.
- Is solution-oriented.

On the mystery shops we conduct, we sometimes hear companies use the term *customer satisfaction*. If all you want is a satisfied customer, you will probably never be as successful as you can be. You need *loyal* customers. You want the move to your community to be the last move your residents will ever make. You must have loyal customers or you can't build a business. So instead of customer satisfaction, let's talk about *customer loyalty.*

Loyalty is not an attribute that occurs when something is wrong or when something is broken. Loyalty comes from doing, and is the result of our doing something positive. Loyalty is an indicator of future business.

When it comes to a relationship with a customer, there are two things in that relationship to care about: Will this customer continue to do business with me? and, Will this customer refer someone else to me? These are measurements of success. How can you know what customers are thinking? One way is to look at the words they use when they talk:

- Happy
- Delighted
- Dynamic
- Wow

Another way of exploring the situation is to look at your own company. How many prospects visited your community last year, but went to live in a competitor's community? In some cases, when they left your tour, you may have believed that these people were satisfied with you. You may offer an excuse, such as XYZ Community had a lower price. In a bit, I am going to share some information that speaks to the exact reasons that prospects go elsewhere.

To define success, consider the word *vulnerable.* All customers are vulnerable to the competition – your competition. This may be coming from leaks of loyalty.

You could consider those lost customers and try to explore the reasoning behind the loss. But instead, challenge yourself to create a game plan that will protect those customers from your competitors. Ask yourself, what are you willing to invest in order to get the best prospects moving in instead of turning to competitors? Will simple satisfaction create the insurance you need to keep these customers from turning to the other guy?

Unfortunately, the answer is no. Your competitors are hoping that your customers are satisfied. This makes those customers vulnerable! In other words, if the competitor's "doing actions" are memorable and value driven, you will lose those customers quickly.

Here is an equation to learn: Having Great Service = Customer Loyalty = Your Service Magic

Some statistics show that it takes ten to thirty times as much work to win a new customer as it does to keep one you already have. Providing your customers with a happy initial experience is going to keep them turning to you and, often more important in the senior community, recommending you to the next person who needs your service.

Get to Know Your Customers

Know them well, more than just who they are or their names. Ask customers questions to learn who they are in life and what they are thinking. While people are quite a bit the same, the preferences, life experiences and personalities of every person are incredibly different.

When you see someone who has just come in to your office, strike up a conversation. If you ask a few questions – and it usually only takes a few – chances are good that this person will open up to you. He will tell you what he needs and what he knows. The more you know about the needs of the customer, the more you can provide a service customized to those needs.

Every Interaction is an Opportunity to Strengthen a Relationship

Another way to work to improve your business success is to make every single interaction with a prospect or potential resident valuable. Let's say that a particular gentleman does not interact well with you on the first visit. He comes in again the next day, though. You are busy, rushing from one appointment to the next. You see him and know a little about what his needs are. Do you stop to talk to him?

It may be easy to rush through the encounter and on to the next pressing thing, but if you take just a few seconds to stop and ask questions, you are building a relationship. Ask how his day is going. Ask how he is doing. Be pleasant, and not rushed. This will translate into improved business success. Now, he knows you are willing to help.

Make absolutely certain that you build rapport with every prospect. I don't care how many trainers have told you not to waste your time on cold leads or those you know will not qualify. You never know when a person will be your next referral source. So remember, every contact is a prospect, and should be treated as such!

Be Happy with the Unlovable

Are you the type of person who is always looking for the easy client – the one who is less hard to persuade or talk to? It often seems that the most challenging customers can turn into the most loyal customers. These loyal customers then become your cheerleaders and best referral sources.

If a new prospect calls you and seems distracted, annoyed, or otherwise obnoxious, it is easy to give the information requested and just hang up. But if you take the time to find out what the caller really needs, chances are good that you can create a relationship that will translate into success down the road.

Pay attention to what the caller is saying. The life experiences of customers like this have often created a belief that unless they are demanding and loud, people, including sales professionals, will not pay attention to them. Many customers who have this "bad attitude" are those who have experienced poor customer service in the past, causing them to believe that all sales professionals are just out to get them.

To deal with these customers and turn them into loyal and enrolled residents, you need to be kind to them. Listen to them. Be friendly and be helpful. In many cases, these are your most valuable customers and will become your most vocal supporters for years to come.

What You Do Matters

What you do and how you do things is a direct reflection of your attitude. As a sales manager, you are responsible for your organization's service culture and for arousing that "delivering magical service" attitude in your staff. **It takes repeated trainings!** Case study discussions and your insistence that problems be handled in the right manner will continue to build trust and loyalty between customers and staff. This will result in excellent customer service.

Chapter 14

Stretch Your Comfort Zone

> *Unless you try to do something beyond what you have already mastered, you will never grow.*
> ~Ralph Waldo Emerson

As soon as we start talking about comfort zones, people start fidgeting in their seats and getting worried, wondering, *What am I going to have to do now?* It is essential to stress the importance of expanding those comfort zones, not simply stepping out of them. Let's be honest about what often happens when seminars begin to focus on *doing* the steps and methods that we *teach*. Here is a look.

I teach a new concept to others. Some may simply not like it or not believe it will work in their business. Or, I teach a new concept, and people are receptive. But, then they go back to the office and do not immediately get the results they want, so they give it up. Some people do see improvements right away, but then tailor what they are doing to make it more "comfortable" for them, retreating back into their comfort zone.

Know this: What I am teaching works. It is proven. It is a technique used by many for the last few years who are seeing incredible results. But to reap the benefits of the program, you will need to accept that this is possible and accept that you need to step out of your comfort zone in order to actually see the benefits.

Do not misunderstand. When learning something new, it is quite common to make mistakes and to downright fail – at first. That is acceptable. However, you need to get right back up and put your big boy pants on and try again. It is not easy, but it is necessary. Ultimate failure happens only when you give up, and at this point, you can no longer do that. In fact, you need to put more focus than ever on improving your sales techniques for the ever-changing world of senior communities. You have to step out of that comfort zone, making that zone bigger, if you are to achieve your goals.

When you do step out of your comfort zone, it will affect you both professionally and personally, and will carry over into other parts of your life. Think of your comfort zone as a big circle surrounding you. Any place you move within that circle you feel at ease, even when you approach the edge. You are content there. Just outside that circle, though, you see a variety of things you are missing, but you are just not able to step outside and grab them. I challenge you to push past the boundary and claim the goods for yourself. Reach out and drag those things into the zone.

How do you do this? By performing activities that you have not done before or do not know how to do well – yet. The key word here is *yet*! That is because when you do them, you will gradually become more comfortable with them.

Stretching is a Must!

Let's take a step back first. Most of us go through life living within our limited range of experiences. Most people are hesitant to explore the new experiences that are out there, and do not want to try things that make them at all uncomfortable.

This "discomfort" zone is one that offers many benefits to you, but for the present, it is outside your reach. It is unfamiliar territory and a place you just do not feel you belong. By contrast, your comfort zone includes life experiences that feel right, normal, safe, and natural.

The comfort zone exists within the subconscious mind. Look at this area of your mind as containing inventory – shelves and shelves of boxes. Each box contains some of your life experiences. All of this is organized or not, but it is full of not only the memory of the experience, but also the memory of the feelings you experienced and the beliefs that stem from those memories. Even your self-image is stored here. As long as something is stored in this warehouse, it is within the comfort zone. Anything not here is out of your reach, it would seem.

Everything that happens to you, your daily experiences and your thoughts, both good and bad, contribute to this subconscious mind. Since your subconscious mind thinks in pictures, you see yourself in pictures. So picture your success.

If you think failure, count on it . . . you will achieve failure.

If you believe you can achieve success, success will be yours.

The single biggest barrier to growth in your personal or professional life is your mind's impact on your behaviors. Whatever is in those boxes is controlling your future, whether you realize it or not. To minimize stress and anxiety, you act within the confines of what is acceptable to your subconscious mind. It seems natural, but it is hurting the way you do business. Most of us are risk averse, and are continuously looking for security. We want to live within an established comfort zone. But living there means missing out.

If you stretch that comfort zone, you will be able to embrace a totally new realm of activities. I don't mean just doing something new, but rather something challenging – a whole new adventure. I'm not talking about trying out a new restaurant where you've never eaten. How about jumping out of a plane, floating to Earth through the clouds?

How many times did you venture into the discomfort zone when you were a child? You climbed trees when you were told not to. You rode down that hill as fast as you could, in the hope of proving your mother wrong when she said you couldn't do it. You explored the creepy neighbor's yard. Perhaps you were the type of kid who would try anything. You could not pass on a dare. Even though you were worried about the consequences of your actions, you ignored your fears and acted anyway. Right?

Unfortunately, too many of us lose that ability to venture into this zone as we get older. If you wander inadvertently into the discomfort zone now, you quickly move back into the comfort zone as soon as you can. The fear of possible failure or embarrassment is so strong that many people find themselves pulling farther and farther away from the edge of that circle.

Attempt to do something new today. What will you feel? Perhaps you want to learn something that has physical danger involved, but there are safety precautions in place. Are you going to jump off a plane in a skydive, or are you going to shudder in terror at the thought, and miss the opportunity? If you do not venture out into the discomfort zone, you will find yourself missing opportunities, both professionally and personally. This is a great misfortune.

The Sales Warrior Pushes Past the Comfort Zone

Think about the sales warrior and the concept of moving into the discomfort zone. When you consider this, realize that a successful sales warrior is not successful just because he is more competent. Successful people push and pull at those boundaries until they stretch them far enough to grab the goods. They stretch their limits and position themselves in the discomfort zone.

Here is a challenge for you: use your comfort zone as a place to rest, not to live.

Re-energize yourself in that zone, but spend the rest of your time working and building yourself into a more successful person in the discomfort zone. The quality of your life really does depend on your ability to do just that. Everyone faces challenges. Challenges force you to move away from the comfort zone, and in doing so, you are forced to experience new things.

There are two methods to consider for the process of expanding your comfort zone:

1. Planned Stretches. The planned stretch is a task that you set for yourself in which you plan to engage in a specific new activity that pushes the bounds, by setting a goal to achieve within a specific timeframe. Write it down.

I will set a goal to do _____ *by the end of the week.*

Fill in that blank. Adhere to the time limit you have set for yourself. Use the SMART method to ensure that your goal is attainable and one that you can make happen. Visualize yourself doing the activity. This will give you time to mentally prepare, and you can envision your success playing out repeatedly in the days leading up to the event.

2. Spontaneous Stretch. It is also a good idea to incorporate an occasional spontaneous stretch into your life. Of course, you cannot plan for this, but you need to be receptive to it when the opportunity arises. Whenever a new opportunity comes up in your daily routine, stretch for it. Do it. Go for it right away.

The less time you spend thinking about the activity, the more time you can take enjoying it. If you wait for the next time, you are missing out. When you take these stretches, don't give yourself time to worry and fret over it. There is no planning, but neither should there be any anxiety.

Make sure you use this second method frequently. From small challenges for yourself to big ones, incorporate spontaneity into your daily life. It will help you become a successful sales warrior.

The Importance of Patience

Most sales entrepreneurs lack patience. You know this. Sometimes, you just want to reach across the table, grab the customer's hand, and help him sign the documents that you know will better his life and yours.

By some statistics, less than five percent of sales are made during the first call with a prospect. About eighty percent are made within five calls. Only ten percent of sales professionals are willing to return for the third phone call.

What does that say? It says that as professionals, we lack the patience and persistence to call again and again and again, as often as necessary.

Most people quit and grumble about not being able to turn sales. Those who are patient and persistent in any industry are the ones who turn into effective, successful professionals. Look at professional athletes. Look at your boss. Success happens over time. Success takes time to build, and if you want to be the type of person who is able to brag to the next guy about the sales you just made, you have to be patient enough to keep trying.

Look around you on your average day, and you will see many quitters. You may be one of them. It hurts, but the fact is, if you are an average person, you often start things and never finish them. Did you learn to play an instrument as a kid? Perhaps you did, and when people ask today, you may say, "I play a little." That may be because you started to learn and stopped. It was boring, dull, or too hard. You quit.

You start an educational program expecting it to change your life, but you quit a few days into it. You start a fitness program, vowing to make it a habit for the rest of your life, but quit before the month is through. You decide to be a sales agent and, just as quickly as anything else, you find the job too hard, and you quit. Only the finest of the fine become successful.

If you are reading this, you could be going down that road. You have a choice to make right now. You can start this training program, implement it, and do well with it by working your tail off to make it happen, or you can quit. If you have a true desire to accomplish more and to be successful, the fact that all of these other people in the room with you are quitters is good news. It makes it easier for you to become successful, because the competition continues to quit.

Think of the millions of people who quit. You do not know their names of course. But you do know the names of those who refused to accept failure as an option and changed their lives for the better. You know names like Thomas Edison, Alexander Graham Bell, Michelangelo, and the Wright brothers.

How does this translate into your business plan? Let's say you call a prospect one time a year. Does that mean you are persistent? Are you persistent if you call a prospect once a week? Yes to both. Just by calling one time per year, you are showing that you haven't forgotten the person. You are telling that customer that you care.

Never give up on a potential customer. Even if customers enroll in another senior center, stay connected. You never know when these people might need to make another housing decision. You want them to think of you when they do.

They could eventually decide to move into your community, because of your patience and caring and persistence.

Suffering from Failure Syndrome?

Do you suffer from Failure Syndrome? If you want to do well in selling, you have to feel successful. It is impossible to move forward when you are struggling mentally, doubting your ability to succeed. If you find yourself trying too hard to sell, you lose the feeling of success. You try to push forcefully through the resistance you are encountering, and that does not lead to a sale. Even the most experienced sales people will do this from time to time.

Instead of allowing this to happen, you need to think from the customer's point of view, considering the customer's objectives. Your job is to solve customers' problems; your customers are people who need real physical and emotional help, in many cases. It is often said that fifty percent of selling is being mentally tough. If you continue to focus on your customers and keep your own feelings in check, the situation will improve. You will hold on to your confidence and relaxed demeanor. You will know what you have to do, and you will know how to do it.

Earlier in this book, we discussed the value of listening. Often the difference between making a sale or not lies in your ability to listen to your prospect when others have not. Turning the sale may require making adjustments to the way you are selling. On the other hand, it may be about getting to the right prospect at the right time.

Did you know that most salespeople who fail during their first year do so because their fears have kept them from doing the prospecting they need to do in order to get the sales numbers that they need? Fears are feelings. You are likely more afraid of your feelings than you are of the actual circumstances leading to those feelings. Anticipation is often worse than actuality. When you find yourself falling prey to your fears, change your focus. Focus your attention outward to the customer and to the customer's responses. Relax and imagine yourself being successful again, recognize the actions that have resulted in past successes, and envision yourself repeating them. The following tips will help you to accomplish just that:

- Solve problems for other people.
- Learn to recognize which words work, and use this knowledge so you can repeat your success.
- Focus on your successes in selling.
- Rehearse your success in your mind, creating a mental image.

Chapter 15

Applying P-Effect to Your Community

> *Greatness is not in where we stand, but in what direction we are moving. We must sail sometimes with the wind and sometimes against it – but sail we must and not drift, nor lie at anchor.* ~Oliver Wendell Homes

You know what the P-Effect system is. Now, you need to apply it to your senior center, assisted living community, or other community. Realize that even in the best of situations, something may go wrong. If you are a true sales warrior, though, when things do go wrong, you will maintain a level head.

Resist the temptation to assign blame for the problem. Blaming others (or yourself) rarely does any good. Focus your energy on getting the problem solved. Remember, when people do poor work, there is a reason behind it. Your plan of action should be to attack the problem, not the person.

When people in your organization need your assistance more than you feel they should, or if they fail to do what you need from them, go to the source and find out why. In some cases, you are going to have to deal with the neediness repeatedly. It is quite common for this to happen to sales managers who have a sales consultant who is in the boss's office day in and day out with a concern, comment, complaint, or problem. As a sales warrior, you need to know how to deal with such people. The only way for a business to do well is for every part of that business to work together toward the same goal. All members need to feel that they can contribute to the team's goal and be an equal and active part of the team.

If you hold a sales leadership position in your company – sales manager, for example – then it is your job to be in contact with the people you are working with. You need to be there and to be interested in them and what they do. Listening is a big part of this process. Do you listen enough? Do you hear what your people are saying and what feelings they are expressing (and implying)? Don't interrupt them when they talk. Don't be shocked by what they say. Don't criticize their feelings or thoughts. If you are tough, critical, and lacking in the ability to connect with those around you, just keep your door shut. Chances are good no one will come to you with concerns anyway.

Here are some things to remember about people, especially those whom you are managing or overseeing.

- Some people rarely complain, while others complain all the time. A complaint is an opportunity to do better.
- Some people know they have it good, but they will always want it better. Most people do.

- Complaints should not bog you down or overwhelm you. They are an opportunity for you to do your job. You are paid to deal with them.
- There is no benefit in fuming about the things that go wrong. Take it in stride, fix it, and move on, knowing you are doing your job.
- The person who is able to learn from the things that go wrong and work through them is winning, in spite of the challenges.

Both Sides and the Company

Whenever a conflict occurs, the best solution is one that benefits both sides, and the business is the winner.

As a manager in a company, you are not better or superior to others in the business. This is a common mistake that many managers make. If you do not notice and appreciate the value of other people and the efforts those people make, you are doing a disservice to the company and to yourself. People are not machines; they need to feel appreciated. In a crisis, people will not help unless they are forced to, if you have treated them as machines. On the other hand, if you show concern for them as people, real human beings, they will feel obliged to help you, and this, in turn, will help the business. Fighting and ill will do not solve any problem.

In your job as a manager, to do your job, you need to work through other people. Your main job is to deal with people, understanding their talents, peculiarities, and temperaments. Managers must be experts in human relations. Your job is to help your team to produce more for the company, in terms of both revenues and good will. Guidance, interest, and appreciation will ensure that every individual on your team is working toward the appropriate goal.

In your organization, is the boss on one side and the workers on another? Is there a distinct line between you, the sales manager, and the sales counselors? Do you feel that you are in an adversarial situation with your workers? This is common, and it leads to problems. When this happens, it creates a division within the team, the team being made up of everyone who contributes to make the business a success. If you are a manager working in a business where there is this type of division, it is up to you to change things. Be aware of what is happening in your organization. Be aware of the way you are interacting with others and how they are interacting with you.

Value is Like Beauty

Like beauty, value is in the eyes of the beholder. It doesn't matter how much you try to sell a prospect on value, if he doesn't see it, you're spinning your wheels. You may think your community is the Taj Mahal of communities, but if the prospect thinks it sucks, then it sucks. Period.

I was coaching a salesperson at a community in Florida. After a three-hour visit that included lunch, the prospect announced that she wanted to research some other places. Here is how the rest of that conversation went:

Salesperson: "You absolutely should visit other communities so you have a comparison. What you are going to find is that our community is the nicest community around."

Prospect: "I kindly disagree. I have seen others that are nicer. They may be a little more expensive, but they are nicer."

Salesperson: "That's true, but do you really want to spend extra money for all those things that are really not that important?"

Prospect: "How do you know they are not important?"

Salesperson: "Well, since you never brought it up in our conversation, I just assumed it was not that important. I know for me, all those bells and whistles don't impress me."

Prospect: "First of all, I did not mention it because you never asked. Second, just because you may not appreciate the finer things does not mean that I do not appreciate them. As a matter of fact, I am willing to pay extra for the bells and whistles, if I think it is worth the money."

The salesperson tried to backpedal, but it was too late. They exchanged their goodbyes, and the salesperson said she would follow up in a few days. Two days later, the prospect did something that is quite off the norm. She called the salesperson back to inform her that she had decided on a different community. Additional follow-up would not be necessary. When asked what community she had decided on, the salesperson was confused – the prospect had moved into a community that was almost identical to hers.

To this day, I still don't think the salesperson gets it. She had given an awesome tour and had a very good chance of closing the deal. Then she made the assumption that what was important to her was shared by the prospect. I don't think she meant any harm. But it doesn't matter what I think or anyone else, other than the prospect.

Perception is Reality

Whether it is perception of yourself or someone else, the cold, hard truth is that perception is each person's reality. When we were conducting our Lost Leads study, one area of research was to determine why prospects did not choose a particular community. The people we interviewed were very nice, for the most part. However, one particular gentleman was quite harsh and very direct. He answered, "I just did not like the lady. She did not talk very much and just asked questions. She did not even ask me if I wanted to live in her community. So, why would I live in a community if I was not welcomed by the staff?"

I knew the salesperson he was referring to, and I had never perceived her as being unwelcoming. She was not much of a talker, but was a great listener. However, she was not a good closer at all. She could have been, but she hardly ever asked. The situation had to be perfect in order for her to ask for the close. If she did not feel it was going well, she simply did not push the matter. So, I called her and asked her if she remembered this man who had come in for the tour that day. Although it had been a year since the tour, she remembered him well when I started describing him. She said, "If you thought he was rude on the phone, you should have seen him in person. There is no reason for anyone to be that mean. However, I was patient and continued my discovery. He is right, though. I didn't ask for the close. I just didn't feel it was the right time, and I didn't want to push him away."

What I did not share with her is that the rude guy really liked the community. He said he would actually have moved in if he had felt welcome. How sad! But it proves the point.

Even though this guy's description of the salesperson was 180 degrees off, it was still his perception. I could have tried talking to him and letting him know what her real personality is like, and that she really did want him to move into the community, but that she just didn't want to come across as pushy. However, I could have talked until I was blue in the face. It would not have made a difference. His mind had been made up. In his eyes, the salesperson was exactly how he perceived her to be, and that was all that mattered. The prospect's perception is his reality, and his opinion is the only one that counts.

Let's take a look how salespeople are perceived in general, as a profession. As we discussed previously, the way many view the sales profession today can be quite negative and disheartening to those of us who make our living in this industry. There will always be a need for sales professionals. Our profession will not be going away. Nevertheless, there has been a shift in the way we identify ourselves to others from sales *persons* to sales *entrepreneurs*. In part, this reflects a change in the way we see ourselves and the way our profession is developing. As the profession develops, our responsibilities are evolving to include greater knowledge of the art and practice of selling. As in any profession, the sales profession will require a professional code of conduct if we are to change public perception of who we are and what we do.

Some salespeople think nothing of the person they are selling to. They do not put time into the sales process. They think only of the onetime sale to pay the bills. These people use the same presentation to everyone who comes in. They just want to survive another day, without a thought to building a strong repeat business model. They expect their future sales to come from promotions the company runs to bring a steady stream of new prospects to the door. This kind of salesperson will never have a secure future. The salesperson who is equipped to survive and thrive is the one who can be flexible and adapt to new business models as well as new types of prospects.

To Change Negative Perceptions, Change Your Mindset

Here is a warning. The Baby Boomer generation is smarter, less likely to tolerate a line of sales talk, and more certain of what they want. If you are planning to use that one dimensional sales approach described above, you are going to fail. People are no longer willing to accept that type of sales presentation, and it will lead you to getting your walking papers. For this reason, you need to change your mindset.

Erase the mindset you have now. Instead of seeing yourself as a salesperson, consider yourself an *entrepreneurial selling professional*. Instead of a one-person sales team, you are a business. If you plan to succeed in this area, you need to be willing and able to apply your sales techniques in a businesslike manner.

Communicate, Communicate, Communicate!

If you consider all the skills and tools at our disposal in the sales industry, there is no doubt that communication skills are the most important. And, yet, these are often the most underdeveloped. Fluent English is not enough. Rather, you need to focus on the needs of others in order to establish a basis for real communication. Understanding behavior styles, which we have already discussed, will give you a good foundation for becoming a master communicator.

The communication process starts with encoding – translating the thoughts initiated in the sender's brain into a verbal message. Then, the receiver must decode the message and try to understand what is being communicated. The message will not be effective unless the receiver accurately interprets the intention behind the message from the sender. If you are a sales counselor sitting with prospective community members, how do you know what they are *really* saying to you?

In selling, communication is more than rattling off a detailed listing of the community's features. There needs to be an active exchange of ideas and thoughts with the prospect. Are you communicating in a two-way exchange with the other person, or are you just reciting a list?

Most salespeople in any given interaction with a customer spend the majority of the time talking. This is wrong. Talking is not enough. Talking too much is a problem, too. The spotlight is on you when you are talking, but you should be doing less talking and more listening. When you listen, you pick up the material you need to lay the foundation of your sales presentation. When you listen, you are able to gather information and learn how you will be able to meet the prospect's needs. Poor listening will cost you that enrollment.

There's No Such Thing as Cold Leads

"I don't have enough leads." "I have worked through all my leads." "I need to go through my database and get rid of the cold leads." "If I have not heard back from them in a year, I don't need to waste my time." If you are a trainer or a coach, you have heard these statements over and over again. Still, no matter how much I train or coach, some people just don't get it. They refuse to change the way they are selling. They would rather whine and make excuses about cold leads than actually put forth some effort.

Well, here is my challenge to you. If you think you have exhausted all of your leads, then start working on your cold leads. Many times, our cold leads are actually our low hanging fruit. That's right; they are actually our hot leads. Because the "cold" prospects have not reached out to us in some time, we store them in the freezer. How many times have you called what was supposedly a cold lead and the prospect's situation just happened to have recently changed? Never happened? That's probably because you have not looked at a cold lead in your database since the Dark Ages. Trust me, it happens all the time. I have personally witnessed it on numerous occasions. I can only imagine how many deals your salespeople would close if I were hovering over the database and forcing them to make these calls. In our Lost Leads study, out of the 500 people we contacted, we had seven who ended up moving into the community. I should have asked for commissions!

Earn the Right

I have said it before, and I will repeat it here: We need to earn the right to ask for the close. Following the steps of the P-Effect sales process will help you earn that right. But remember the rule, though: even if you have not earned the right to ask for the close, ask anyway. Always ask for the close.

If prospects come in and ask for information about your community, and you do what most salespeople do and throw up on their shoes (go into presentation mode), you are no different from the other ninety-five percent of salespeople. Why should they trust you any more than they trust your competitors? No reason at all! You have to give them a reason to trust you. Remember, prospects don't care how much you know until they know how much you care.

Build rapport with the prospect – every prospect. Picture this: You are on one side of the Grand Canyon, and the prospect is on the other side. Hovering in the middle of the Grand Canyon is Trust. You must start building that bridge between you and Trust before the prospect will ever take a step. When the prospect sees you genuinely moving toward Trust, then and only then will he begin to bridge the gap as well. Once you meet in the middle, you have earned the right to be right. In the eyes of the prospect, you are no longer trying to sell him. You are trying to help him come to the solution that will work best.

So, how will you know when you have earned the right to be right? There is no doubt in my mind that you will know. You and your prospect will have an experience that neither of you has often experienced. The prospect will visually display his emotions when buying, and you will find yourself caring more about those emotions than about the paycheck the sale will bring.

Start earning the right to be right and transform your sales process into an event that is almost impossible to put into words. Be the transformation that you want to see.

Waiting Lists

Companies love to brag when they are 100% occupied with a waiting list. I have one word of advice for you. *Beware!*

As rewarding as it may be having a full building, you are entering the danger zone. Salespeople become complacent. Managers become lazy. Executives cut back on staff development budgets. Then it happens: All of a sudden, your community loses fifteen or twenty residents in the course of two months. Everyone begins to scramble. The sirens are blaring. There seems to be a sales meeting every day. You are now in catch-up mode.

I compare catch-up mode to pain management. I have had a number of surgeries in my life, including eleven on my knees. I learned a lesson on pain management very early. After my first knee surgery, I was sent home with a nice supply of pain medication. I was sixteen years old and tough as nails (or so I thought). The anesthesia from a surgery tends to linger for several hours, so, since I was feeling no pain at first, I did not take my medication. I was thinking this surgery thing was a piece of cake. Then it hit me.

The pain increased gradually for just a short time, then it seemed as if my brain activated every nerve in my body and opened up the floodgates of my senses. The pain rushed in, and it was excruciating. I started taking my pain medications, but I was in catch-up mode. The pain had a huge jump on me. It took the entire night and into the following day before I was able to get the pain to a moderate level. It only took that single incident to teach me my lesson.

Just like pain management, when our buildings are full with a waiting list, we think this job is a piece of cake. We may even snicker at our competitors who are struggling. Life is good, and we are "chilaxing" (chilling and relaxing). Then the bottom drops out.

The first place we go is to our wait list. That will be the life preserver. Then we realize the wait list is not very accurate. Most of the people on the wait list have decided to move to different communities. Some have changed their minds about our community and now live at one of our competitors' communities. Sure, we collected a deposit, but the competitor probably gave them a big enough discount that they recouped the lost deposit. You see, we tend to forget the prospects who go on a wait list. However, a handful of salespeople do a real job of following up. The prospect's situation changed, and your competitor was there with a solution.

If we've been doing our due diligence and continuing with the same habits that got our building full, this will be a piece of cake. If we have become lazy and complacent, it is too late. Our salespeople have forgotten how to sell. Most of us suck at following up. Yes, I said we suck. It may be harsh, but it drives the point home. While we scramble around like chickens with our heads cut off, we are losing a ton of money with empty apartments.

So, salespeople and managers, if you have a wait list, I congratulate and envy you. Just continue to do what made you successful. Don't cut back on staff development. As a matter of fact, if you are full, you have the financial resources to afford it. Would you like to know my thoughts on this? I hope so, because since I am the author, I have the floor. Whether you have a full building or not, you simply cannot afford *not* to continue developing your staff. If you do not care about staff development, then stop whining about lost revenue when the bottom drops out.

Turn the danger zone into your reward zone. Continue to build on the same ideas and habits that got you to where you are. Then when the bottom drops out, recovery really will be a piece of cake.

Let's say you have done everything perfectly. You followed the P-Effect sales process exactly as trained. However, the prospect still walks. Now what? Well, we know we are not going to close everyone who walks through the door. Your job is not over. On the contrary, it has just begun. It's time to start your creative follow-up – creative being the operative word in this sentence. If you are sending out the same boring draft emails, letters, and brochures, you might as well not even bother following up. Stop wasting your time and money, and killing off earth's natural resources.

If you are going to take the time to follow up, then make it worth the prospect's while. Personalize the email and letter. Take the information you learned and use it as a tool to keep in touch with your prospects. The key is persistence. When should you stop following up? Never! If they ask you to stop following up, it's because they are tired of getting your junk mail. If you ensure the follow up is personal, who would want you to stop? The prospects will not want you to stop, but you will stop anyway. Statistics have proven it, and the numbers don't lie.

The Slot Machine Syndrome

The premise of the "Slot Machine" syndrome is that the average sales representative gives up after only three or four calls to a potential customer. However, we know that eighty percent of sales are closed after five calls, but only ten percent of representatives ever make the third call. Not too long ago, I spoke to a friend who visits casinos regularly. She has done very well with the "one-armed bandits." Her winning percentages far outweigh her losses. So, I inquired about her strategy. She graciously opened up and revealed her "secret." Her slot machine strategy works something like this: She walks into a casino. She immediately goes to the slot machine area and begins "slot watching." She looks for those people who are relaxed and appear to have been at a machine for a while. She observes if the machine has paid out, and how much. Then she exercises her patience. As tempting as it is to get in the game, she observes. She hears the sounds of clinking coins as they hit the coin tray, but she waits. She hears the sound of bells as others win a few aisles over, but she waits and observes. Sometimes she waits thirty minutes. Other times she has been known to wait an hour or two. Sometimes she even sits next to a person and strikes up a conversation with the gambler about the winnings. Eventually, the person gets up and leaves, no longer able take the losses at that slot machine. There has to be another slot in this casino that will pay out. So, the person walks away. And my friend, who has been lying in the tall grass like a lion stalking its prey, leaps to the empty chair. She knows that the current person just dumped a huge amount of money into this machine – maybe an entire paycheck or this month's mortgage payment. The current "slotter" did all the work. Just a few spins later, my friend wins a nice lump sum of money. Does it work all the time? No. Does it work many times? Yes.

Are You Handing Over Deals to Your Competitors?

Let's apply the Slot Machine Theory to your community. You make the first call and the second call, generating some interest from the customer. After the third call, the customer may not be sold yet, but is probably interested. You have piqued his interest to maybe eighty percent. However, having made your two or three calls, you give up, moving on to the next potential customer. Once again, the desire for instant gratification prevails and sabotages the sale. Your competitor shows up shortly after you abandoned the customer and simply gave up. The customer, still at an eighty percent level of interest, now entertains your competitor's proposal. How much selling did your competitor have to do? Only twenty percent! Gottcha! You just handed that sale to your competitor on a silver platter. He or she should send you a thank-you note saying, "Thanks for giving up. Have a nice day."

My question to you is this: How many potential accounts are you working on where you may be exposed to the Slot Machine Syndrome? You'd better check it out. How often have you given up on a customer relationship, only to later discover that your competitor, who was more persistent, got the sale? It's frustrating and unnecessary. The attitude of persistence will not eliminate the Slot Machine Syndrome entirely, but it will certainly help minimize it. Stay focused on the accounts that will truly contribute to your business, even if it takes a year or two to close them.

Does Practice Make Perfect?

You have heard the saying *practice makes perfect*, but it is not completely true. In fact, you could find yourself practicing the wrong thing and ending up becoming perfect at doing it incorrectly. So, does practice *really* make perfect? Before you answer, let me share a thought.

I love to golf. I started playing when I was fourteen years old. I was horrible. I was always athletically inclined, but golf was kicking my butt. I never took any lessons as I was learning to play. In my twenties, I began to play more often. I went to the driving range several days a week to practice.

There was a time when I played three or four times a week. I got pretty good. I was actually shooting about five or six strokes over par. Ask any golfer you know. Many of us hackers never reach that level.

So, I was feeling pretty good about my golf. I had found a way to make my game work for me. Still, I wanted to be even better. So, I finally broke down and took a lesson. The first thing the pro did was adjust my grip. He called it strengthening my grip. He had me rotate my hands just a slight bit clockwise on the shaft of the club. I was hosed. That threw my entire game off. I was ticked. I tried it for a few weeks, but the progress was simply not happening quickly enough. I had developed such bad habits that the slightest correction changed the entire game for me. I had spent numerous hours practicing, but I was practicing the wrong way. I had created bad habits. No matter how much I practiced the wrong way, I was not going to get any better. I had reached the peak of my game. Had I stuck with what the professional trainer had told me and practiced that, I would probably be a much better golfer today.

Can we apply my golfing lesson to the principles of selling? I am almost ready for your answer, but let me add one word and see if that changes your perspective. Perfect practice makes perfect. You may spend eight hours a day practicing your selling skills, but if they are not the correct skills, you are practicing in vain. So, what are you practicing? This is where coaching and training come in.

Practicing your skills in handling inquiries is important. It is something that sales managers should do in a group format, with role-playing. You need to practice the right procedures in the right order to really make a difference in your profit margin. No matter how much you practice, you must practice perfect skills. If you practice the wrong procedures and steps, you are only going to find yourself making mistakes when you talk to actual prospects. Once the mystery shops are complete and you have identified where you need to practice, then start practicing the right way. The dividends will be huge.

Practicing is only the start, though. Learn the P-Effect methodology. Incorporate the information we have provided in this book. Use the same process each time, tailoring that system to fit your particular prospect.

Chapter 16

Are You a Winner?

> *I firmly believe that any man's finest hours –*
> *his greatest fulfillment of all that he holds dear –*
> *is that moment when he has worked his heart out*
> *in good cause and lies exhausted on the field*
> *of battle – victorious.* ~Vince Lombardi

There are two types of people in the world – those who win and those who do not. Which one do you think you are? Now answer this: Which one are you? This is a question answered by perception. Your attitude and your actions will determine whether you are a winner or not. Closing more deals does not make you a winner. Higher bonuses do not make you a winner. Plaques, trophies, and other accolades do not make you a winner. What you do to prepare and how you perform based on your preparation is what makes you a winner.

In the senior living industry, winning is not about getting your prospect to sign on the bottom line and make them future residents. That is the bonus in winning. Winning in this industry is doing everything within our power to help future residents – whether they become our residents or not. Your greatest competition is not the surrounding communities – it is yourself. The war that must be won is not on the battlefield or on a field. The war that must be won is a series of battles that are waged against our own practices and beliefs.

More about Attitude

We already considered the importance of a Doing Attitude. I'd like to expand our discussion of attitude here, because no matter what we do, our attitude is our driving force in life. Countries lose wars oftentimes because they lose their will to fight. In other words, their attitude went from *I can* to *I can't*.

Countless books have been written about having the "right attitude." I just went to Amazon.com and typed in "attitude," and a list of 39,186 books was displayed within seconds. Over the years, I have read many books about attitude, and all of the authors agree: *Your attitude determines your altitude!*

Attitude determines your destiny, quality of life, and sales success. The quality of your attitude affects the quality of your life. These are profound statements but true. The proficiencies found in today's sales arena go far beyond selling skills. Attitude is one of these proficiencies. Without it, all other skills are handicapped. Attitude is what drives the practice of skills. Extensive product knowledge alone affords you little advantage if your attitude is one of indifference or if you lack belief in yourself.

As you develop in your sales career, you will be inundated with product knowledge, company policies and procedures, price manuals, and other tools of the trade. People often lose sight of the human side of selling. Why does the sales profession complicate such a fundamental process? We put on our business attire Monday morning, then proceed to divorce ourselves from the human aspect of our profession. We become "robot-reps" guided by a mechanical process. Through a positive attitude, you can refocus and develop a humanized approach with your customers.

A positive attitude will transform an average sales profession into a top performer. It empowers you to achieve new levels of success both personally and professionally. Winners choose to nurture and develop a positive, winning attitude. They understand the importance of a winning edge and use it to differentiate themselves in their own personal lives and with their customers. Attitude provides that edge. People prefer to deal with winners. You are selling to people. Are you a winner?

The normal implementation of a training program begins with two days of P-Effect sales training to the group, and then a follow-up session about forty-five to sixty days later. After the second training session, I begin to coach at the community level and help the salespeople identify their unique selling style.

Several months ago, I began working with a company that managed a handful of communities. The group training was welcomed by most of the team, with a couple of exceptions. It was obvious to everyone in the room that the walls of defense were up. I was not surprised, as I see this with most new clients. It was a small challenge, and I love challenges.

The coaching at the community level seemed to be going very well. We were picking up momentum and were seeing changes. It was easy to point out the salespeople who were hungry for more knowledge. Those were the ones who emailed and called me at least on a weekly basis. These were not people who were new to the industry or new to sales. They were successful people who had a desire for more knowledge and knew they could always be better. Although people like this are few and far between, they are the ones that give me the motivation to pack my bags every week, get on a plane, and fly all over the country. It's the others who drain me of my energy.

I had spent a couple days at a particular community and left feeling very good. It was my first visit, and I felt I had gained the trust of the sales staff. I train my clients that they need to gain the trust of their prospects so the prospects will be honest with them. When they are trustful, the prospects will share their true emotions. I take the same approach with my clients. I do not want to be looked at as the eyes and ears of the home office. I want the people I'm working with to trust that I am there to help.

In this case, my perception was that I had gained some ground and earned their trust. My report back to the home office was very positive. I was expecting some great things from this team. It was after I arrived back home that I found out differently. The details do not matter, but it was obvious that the staff at that community had gone on the defensive. I knew that I was not going to be able to work with that community again as long as that sales team was in place. I also knew that my client would have to conduct his own research to determine the validity of the issues. After a long email and a short conversation, we made the decision to put the training on hold.

It is the attitude of people like those mentioned above that poisons a community and company. As a result, the salespeople from the other communities suffer. The company will leave thousands of dollars on the table because change will not happen. It is a ripple effect. The sad part is that the staff at that community feels victorious. They get to continue doing what they have been doing and will not be held accountable. Eventually, the truth will come out and the company will demand accountability. But in the meantime, everyone loses, because a couple of people had the wrong attitude.

A result like this affects us more than we give credit to. This incident sucked the energy right out of me. I knew beyond any doubt that great opportunities were possible at this community, and as a team, we were going to make strides quickly. Helping salespeople is what I do. This is my calling. I felt as if I had failed. The key is not to train ourselves to be successful, but to train ourselves on how to fail. When we accept failure as part of the learning process, then ultimate failure does not become an option. I will take this incident and learn from it. Does that mean it doesn't hurt? Absolutely not. On the contrary, I take my job very personally. So, it hurts like you know what.

Nevertheless, I will drive on. I am a winner, but that does not mean I never lose. That is my choice. That is my attitude.

Instant Gratification = Constant "Wreckification"

Instant gratification is one of the primary reasons why salespeople fail. If you have recently changed industries and started a career in the senior living industry, this will be one of your biggest challenges. Even for some who have spent their entire career in the senior living industry face this particular demon every day. I personally believe it is just part of our human nature. However, it's still not an excuse.

Instant gratification will result in lost deals. If you attempt to rush the sales cycle, you are going to lose the majority of your prospects. You cannot forget that this is a life changing event for your prospect. This is an emotional struggle that they have been battling for months – sometimes even years.

The key is to be patient. However, if you have built a relationship with the prospect and have earned the right to be heard, then you have earned the right to help the prospect move to a closing posture. The key is earning the right. You see, not only do we have to earn the right to be heard, we have to earn the right to be right.

If you are a manager of a sales team, you are doing no favors to them by pressuring them to get the close. If you think you can get the close any quicker, then go do it. Turn it into a training opportunity. If the salesperson is doing the best they can, then ease up. I know you are getting pressure from your boss. It is your job as a leader to be the buffer so your team can sell without the pressure. Saying that, if you have provided the resources and the environment for that salesperson to be successful and they are just not "making the cut," then it is time for you to make the cut. Accountability is a two way street though. Make sure you look into the mirror prior to making any cuts!

We have talked about attitude and how much of an influence it has on the success of the sales process. Instant gratification has a direct correlation to the attitude and motivation of the salesperson. Selling is a roller coaster ride of emotions. Sometimes we are up and sometimes we are down. When a salesperson's efforts do not pay off quickly enough, even the fully capable salespeople seem to get discouraged. When managers start feeling the heat, they pass along that pressure. When a salesperson feels more pressure than the norm, they begin to sell differently. They take the focus off of the prospect and turn it towards themselves. This is a no win situation.

If you genuinely care about your prospects, you need to stay on their agenda. This means you must stop feeling like the deal should close when you want it to close. When an instant gratification environment is created, you are not selling and the prospect is not buying. So, regardless of the amount of pressure that is applied, your efforts will be in vain.

The bottom line is that a good leader will also be a good manager. Ensure the sales process focuses on our prospects and not on us. That means that managers are going to have to do what their title says – manage. Be accountable and hold others accountable. It is necessary to closely manage the sales process. However, before the sales process can be managed, it must be manageable.

If you were manufacturing a product, would you have systems in place to monitor, control, and improve the product? So, why do we not have these quality control measures in place for our selling system? Successful organizations do have these quality control measures in place. They are continuously monitoring and measuring the sales process and how it is being adhered to. These companies continue to follow up with these control measures and following through with continuous training and coaching. It is a financial investment, but the return is great. That's what makes them successful.

Can You Feel It?

The first step in selling is feeling successful. You can't lead a cavalry charge if you think you look funny sitting on a horse. Salespeople who feel successful help everyone around them share those feelings. That develops trust, a key factor in selling.

Salespeople lose the feeling of success the moment they try too hard to sell their ideas, when they try to push their ideas through resistance. Even experienced salespeople sometimes forget that selling is problem solving, meeting other people's needs as well as their own.

Sales begin with the customer's objectives, not with the product. Selling requires thinking from the customer's viewpoint, and always thinking in terms of solving problems for the customer. Mental toughness is fifty percent of selling. Salespeople need to create and maintain the right kind of focus and feelings, regardless of the situation or the obstacles they encounter. If you sustain feelings of confidence and relaxation, you can stay focused on the customer. You'll know what to do and when to do it.

The difference between success and failure in making a sale is often as small as listening when others don't, making a slight adjustment in your selling style, or getting to the right prospect at the right time. When these small differences are repeated consistently, they add up to peak performance.

Some authors suggest selling is a numbers game: talk to ten people, get five presentations, close two deals. That sounds like a lot of work – not selling very smart. It bears out the fact that the average close ratio is only twenty percent. That means, on the average, salespeople close only two out of ten potential opportunities. Funny, I always thought selling was about people, not a game with winners, losers, and average or mediocre performances. Don't fall victim to the numbers game, condemning your career to mediocrity. Don't measure your success against the masses. By comparing yourself against the averages, you only fuel a false sense of productivity. Set your own standards. Don't take pride in being average – it's too easy and not very satisfying.

How to Double Your Closing Ratios

Remember that confirming (not necessarily "The Close,") is not an event, but a process that begins within minutes of meeting the customer. Customers are very quick to pass judgment, and waste no time deciding if you are likable and trustworthy. The first step to doubling your close ratio is to ensure the first steps of your P-Effect model have been completed to the customer's satisfaction. You can literally make or break the sale in the first five minutes.

If closing ratios are a mere twenty percent, that means the customers' ratio is eighty percent. Ouch! Customers are closing more often than we are. They sell us on the concept of not doing business with them. They offer a multitude of excuses, objections, and justifications, all in the interest of selling us their no. The problem is that we are too quick to accept their rejection, and with bruised egos, we return to our offices to lick our wounds. Sound familiar?

So, what is a good close ratio? I would suggest your target should be no less than forty or fifty percent. That means if you approach ten potential customers, ones with a need and a bag of money, you should confirm at least four or five. Sound daunting? It isn't. Some top-notch sales warriors are confirming up to seventy-five percent of potential customers. How are they doing it?

You cannot expect what you do not inspect. Start by evaluating your current ratio. Track it for a month or two and reality will quickly reveal itself. It may not be as high as you think it is. If yours is higher than twenty percent, congratulations, you are in the minority. I will remind you, your objective is forty to fifty percent. Proper execution of your P-Effect model will certainly contribute to doubling your current close ratio. It simply means building rapport and trust as you navigate through the first steps of the model, coupled with having the confidence to ask for the prospect's business. Customers expect to be asked; don't disappoint them. You represent a solution to their needs, so the only outstanding issue is to ask. If you don't, someone else will – and will be rewarded with a bag of money that could have been yours. So, taking your close ratio to forty percent is not an impossible or arduous objective.

Are You Looking Through the Eyes of Your Customer?

I now want to reiterate the benefits of a mystery shopping program. As I previously mentioned in the book, many companies worry about marketing and getting leads into the door, yet they fail to focus on how to convert those leads. The thousands of dollars that are being left on the table is almost unspeakable. And very seldom do sales managers point those numbers out.

There are numerous benefits to a mystery shopping program. Regardless of how tight your budget is, you still have room to at least conduct the telephone mystery shops. For around $40.00 a month, you could eliminate many missed opportunities. Remember, eighty percent of the deals are lost over the phone because our salespeople cannot get the caller in the door. These are some key areas that you will immediately identify with a mystery shopping program: Rapport building is simply not taking place. The salesperson believes that selling is telling and goes into presentation mode within the first two minutes of the call. Rarely are open ended questions used at all. As a matter of fact, you will probably discover that the salesperson asks very few questions. Those questions they ask normally revolve around the prospect's medical condition, how they heard about the community, and their contact information.

Sending a brochure is the typical close and the answer to most objections. Rarely does the salesperson capture the prospect's email address either. Over seventy percent of Independent Living prospects are online and obtain their information on the Internet. For Assisted Living and higher care levels, it is normally the adult child who is looking for a place for the parent, and over ninety-eight percent of those prospects are online.

Salespeople are doing a better job of asking prospects to come in for a tour. However, the close is at the wrong time. They often ask in the very beginning of the call, before they have had the opportunity to go through the sales process. They think they are hitting a home run, but they have never left home plate. When the prospects shoot them down, they attempt to recover by going into presentation mode.

The salesperson should be talking about twenty percent of the time and listening the other eighty percent. The exact opposite is happening. I have listened to thousands of mystery shops. I actually get a little excited when I hear the salesperson only talking about sixty percent of the time.

This takes us back to the kind of questions that are being asked.

The prospects ask the majority of the questions. The salesperson answers a question and then moves on, without taking the opportunity to explore why the question was asked.

Rarely (five percent or less) does the sales agent ask questions regarding the feelings of the prospect. The questions are mostly logic based. Rarely do we ask who is involved in the decision. This should happen between first and second base.

I mentioned that rapport building is a consistently weak area. If it is the adult child calling in, the salesperson is not building rapport with the adult child at all. Diving in and asking about Mom or Dad's medical condition is not a sign that we actually care. Remember, the person calling in or coming to visit is probably one of the main decision-makers.

When you implement your own mystery shopping program, I am sure you will see these missed opportunities, along with many others. I have never listened to a mystery shop where I was unable to find a training opportunity. Ninety-five percent of salespeople in the industry are making these mistakes. If you are reading this book, chances are you or and your team of salespeople fall into this group. Is it worth $40.00 a month to be able to double your closing ratios? The obvious answer is yes, although the majority of you will not take action. That's good news for those who do, though. You will get eighty percent of the business, while the others are competing for the rest.

The "Phil" Factor

A couple of years ago, I was invited to give a three hour presentation to a senior living community on the east coast. I was invited to dinner the night before to meet all of the salespeople who would be at my seminar. I always welcome the opportunity to meet with attendees prior to any speaking engagement, regardless of the length of the presentation.

As we sat around the dinner table, one discussion lead to another and eventually we were talking about our families. The lady sitting directly to my right made a statement about her husband Phil. Before she had a chance to go into the story any further, all of the other ladies began to talk about how wonderful Phil is and how lucky Michelle was to have him as a husband. They could not say enough about Phil. They even went as far to say who was going to get to marry Phil next. I was so glad my wife was not there, because Phil has definitely raised the bar when it comes to husbands. By the end of the night, I was ready to marry Phil! Ok, my marrying Phil is quite the stretch, but I think you get the point. Just being around Phil sounds like it would make you want to be a better person.

You can imagine everyone's surprise the following morning when I added the Phil Factor to the presentation. What if we could create a Phil Factor effect in our communities? What if our prospects walked out the door and shared with everyone they met how wonderful your community is and how they cannot wait to move in? What if prospects were lining up to move into the "Phil Factor" community? That would be awesome, right? Is it possible though?

Creating the "Phil Factor" effect in your community is not only possible, but a reality. It is up to you to own the possibility! It is not going to just happen. You have to make it happen. Just listening to the Phil stories, I wondered what the percentages of relationships had a "Phil" in them – the spouse that could do no wrong. My thoughts were maybe 1 in 100 or even 1 in 1000. Who knows? My next thought was how many communities have the Phil Factor effect in their communities? I cannot accurately place a number or percentage on the answer to that question, but I can say without any reservation that there are very few Phil Factor communities.

What does it take to become a Phil Factor community? It takes the entire organization working together as a team. The efforts of one team player mean very little if synergy does not exist. It must be a team effort. However, it starts with you – the salesperson. You are the captain of this team and should be championing the effort to transform your community into a Phil Factor community. You have to be the leader. More than anything else, you have to want it – and you have to want it more than anyone else. It won't be about doing what your competitors are doing. It will be about doing what others do not do. It starts with being genuinely concerned with the prospect and those people in their lives. When you stop selling and start caring, the transformation will begin.

Final Notes

You have reached the end of the book. Perhaps you have learned something that you can apply in your community today. Perhaps you are like many "experts" who know all the facts and have excelled in your respective fields. Perhaps this book was simply a review of what you already know.

Whether it is new material or a refresher, one thing we all should have learned is that sales skills are perishable. If we do not use them, we lose them. You need to consistently polish your skills or they will soon lose their shine.

Application of the strategies and techniques of the P-Effect model enables you to navigate with confidence through the entire sales call, steadily moving your customer toward a buying decision. Your completed P-Effect model is a continuous loop, guiding you through every aspect of the relationship, with each completed step setting up the next. Your biggest challenge now will be to unlearn cherished old sales habits and to embrace the new techniques outlined in the P-Effect model.

I share with you a comment from a very successful sales warrior: "You beat fifty percent of the salespeople in North America just by working hard. You beat another forty percent by being a person of honesty and integrity. The last ten percent is a dogfight in the free enterprise system." I agree. His comment is a strong reminder of the importance of embracing an entrepreneurial code of conduct, guided by your P-Effect model. As you travel on your journey, I ask you to ponder the following points: Change is a prerequisite to success. Learning is a sequential process, marked by stages of growth and development. Learning is cumulative. Perfect practice is the key.

Stop Selling and Start Caring!

CPSIA information can be obtained at www.ICGtesting.com
Printed in the USA
BVOW06s1158201016

465449BV00008B/145/P